FLORIDA STANDARDS

A Handbook for Teaching in the Sunshine State

Susan Nelson Wood

Florida State University

Upper Saddle River, New Jersey
Columbus, Ohio

Library of Congress Cataloging-in-Publication Data
Wood, Susan Nelson
    Florida standards : a handbook for teaching in the Sunshine State / Susan Nelson Wood.
      p. cm.
    Includes bibliographical references and index.
    ISBN 0-13-119391-0
    1. Teaching—Florida—Handbooks, manuals, etc.   2. Teachers—Training of —Florida—
Handbooks, manuals, etc.   I. Title
LB1775.3.F6W66 2007
379.1'58—dc22

2006015710

Vice President and Executive Publisher: Jeffery W. Johnston
Executive Editor: Debra A. Stollenwerk
Senior Editorial Assistant: Mary Morrill
Assistant Development Editor: Daniel J. Richcreek
Production Editor: Kris Roach
Production Coordination: Techbooks
Design Coordinator: Diane C. Lorenzo
Cover Designer: Bryan Huber
Cover image: Super Stock
Production Manager: Susan Hannahs
Director of Marketing: David Gesell
Senior Marketing Manager: Darcy Betts Prybella
Marketing Coordinator: Brian Mounts

This book was set in Minion Roman by *Techbooks*. It was printed and bound by R.R. Donnelley &
Sons Company. The cover was printed by Phoenix Color Corp.

Pearson Prentice Hall™ is a trademark of Pearson Education, Inc.
Pearson® is a registered trademark of Pearson plc
Prentice Hall® is a registered trademark of Pearson Education, Inc.
Merrill® is a registered trademark of Pearson Education, Inc.

Pearson Education Ltd.
Pearson Education Singapore Pte. Ltd.
Pearson Education Canada, Ltd.
Pearson Education—Japan

Pearson Education Australia Pty. Limited
Pearson Education North Asia Ltd.
Pearson Educación de Mexico, S.A. de C.V.
Pearson Education Malaysia Pte. Ltd.

PEARSON
Merrill
Prentice Hall

10 9 8 7 6 5 4 3 2 1
ISBN: 0-13-119391-0

Preface

Good teaching cannot be reduced to technique; good teaching comes from the identity and integrity of the teacher.

Parker J. Palmer

Florida Standards: A Handbook for Teaching in the Sunshine State is a supplemental text for elementary and secondary preservice teachers preparing to teach and inservice teachers already teaching in Florida's schools. Focusing specifically on Florida, almost with a hometown feel, the discussion uses the language, resources, and policies that currently exist in the Sunshine State.

At the heart of the book is a focus on student learning. In the domains of learning, school demographics, student needs, and curricular variance, this book is meant to provide readers with an increased understanding of how to make a difference in the classroom.

It is no secret that Florida—like many states in the first decade of the new century—is experiencing a critical shortage of qualified teachers, and the number of teachers needed each year grows far more quickly than the number being prepared. Consequently, talented individuals are being recruited for classrooms at all levels, and as new teachers are hired, they discover they have questions about how to be an effective classroom leader.

This book is intended to serve as a resource for anyone interested in learning more about standards-based learning, especially for readers preparing to teach in Florida. Rather than being limited to a specific discipline or certification level, the book will appeal to all teachers (K–12) and those in all academic areas—not just a math methods course or an English language arts workshop, but across all courses and learning opportunities, in all kinds of teacher education and preparation programs, and for those with varied professional development experiences.

Organization

As identified in Figures 1, 2, and 3 in the Introduction, this book begins with an emphasis on outcomes. The three foci are candidate knowledge, skill, and dispositions. After reading the book, students will know more about teaching and learning in a standards-based system, be able to monitor their professional development, and be better equipped to define their personal philosophy of teaching and learning.

Each of the six chapters in *Florida Standards: A Handbook for Teaching in the Sunshine State* targets specific performance indicators, or objectives designed to meet the book's

Matrix. Alignment of Chapter Objectives to the *Florida Educator Accomplished Practices (FEAP)*

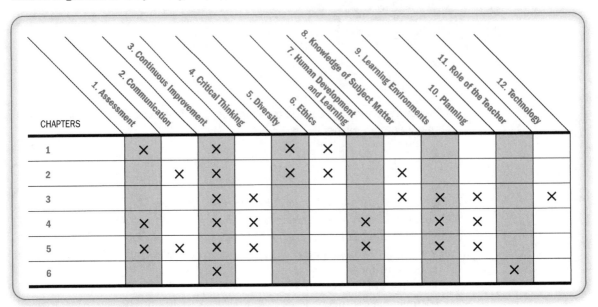

CHAPTERS	1. Assessment	2. Communication	3. Continuous Improvement	4. Critical Thinking	5. Diversity	6. Ethics	7. Human Development and Learning	8. Knowledge of Subject Matter	9. Learning Environments	10. Planning	11. Role of the Teacher	12. Technology
1	X		X			X	X					
2		X	X			X	X		X			
3			X	X					X	X	X	X
4	X		X	X				X		X	X	
5	X	X	X	X				X		X	X	
6			X								X	

goals, and each chapter is also aligned with the 12 "accomplished practices" that guide teacher learning in Florida (see the matrix above). The book is based on the premise that teachers who make a difference accept full responsibility for student learning and thus develop evidence-based, reflective habits used to advocate for the success of all students.

Special Features

- **Outcome expectations.** Goals and objectives for readers are presented in Figures 1, 2, and 3 in the Introduction and at the start of each chapter.
- **Reflective prompts.** To support readers as they monitor and self-assess, a series of reflective prompts are placed throughout the book.
- **Before reading.** As a window into the complex issues addressed in this book, *Taking a Stance* boxes are placed at the beginning of each chapter. The open-ended statements invite readers to consider their positions and opinions before reading. They also encourage collaborative discussions.
- **During reading.** *Informing Your Stance* and *Articulating Your Stance*, mid-chapter checkpoints, are boxes that appear throughout each chapter, prompting further thinking, writing, and discussion.
- **After reading.** Toward the end of each chapter, *Researching Your Stance* and *Extending Your Stance*, two series of questions, prompt readers to review initial assumptions and offer suggestions for further research.

- **Demonstrating learning.** Each chapter ends with a summary containing questions aligned with the chapter's objectives. In addition, all writing completed during the reading of this book will document student learning and, if chosen, may serve as artifacts in a professional portfolio.
- **Resources.** Because of the constant shifts in standards and assessments, the primary resources offered in this book are Internet links. Web sites have been carefully selected to provide the kind of specificity impossible to contain in this brief book.
- **Glossary.** The specialized vocabulary of the standards movement as applicable to this book is defined in a short glossary.

ACKNOWLEDGMENTS »

I wish to thank several key people without whom I would not have proceeded. You see, this is not a book I wanted to write. Like many veteran classroom teachers, I have been dismayed by the politicization of education. Given my commitment to teacher education, to long-term teacher development, and to the professionalization of classroom teachers, I was uncomfortable writing a book about contentious issues. Worse, I was afraid to perpetrate some of the damaging practices currently at work in our school system.

The writing of this book was fueled by the passion, concerns, and talent of the following people:

- Thanks to the courage of teachers at all levels: those caught in the middle, those braving the accountability demands, and those who care deeply, who want to know better how to think clearly, and who demand resources to help their students succeed.
- Thanks especially to Chuck Glaeser, Julie Langston, Kristin Mudd, Tameka King, and other classroom teachers who shared their experiences.
- Thanks to the giants, my teachers, like Miles Myers, Eliot Wigginton, Jonathan Kozol, and so many other caring people, who continually remind me that reform initiatives do matter. Standards-based models can make a difference when we pay attention and remain vigilant. The data collected as the result of the No Child Left Behind Act, for example, illuminate the growing national crisis concerning equity issues for children living in poverty, for those coping with other disabling circumstances, and for racial and language minorities.
- Thanks to the K–12 students who do not give up, who hope each summer that next year's teachers will know enough and care enough to help them succeed.
- Thanks to the new breed of teachers, those who enter classrooms with love in their hearts, understanding the art as well as the science of teaching, as well as the power of literacy, technology, and human relationships to change lives.
- Thanks to the parents, and citizens everywhere, who continue to listen to educators and who believing in the work of teachers, vote accordingly.

- Thanks to the warmth and support of my colleagues, especially Sissi Carroll, Shari Steadman, and all those in the Department of Middle and Secondary Education at Florida State University who continue to ask the hard questions and do not settle for easy answers.
- Thanks to the urging of Ben Stephen, who recognized that the acute shortage of teachers in Florida necessitated a different kind of textbook, to Debbie Stollenwerk and Mary Morrill for helping me get it done, and to Helen Greenberg for her careful editing.
- Thanks to all those who reviewed early drafts of the manuscript: Henri Sue Bynum, Indian River Community College; Susan Caldwell, Palm Beach Community College; Pat Daniel, University of South Florida; Mark J. Guillette, Valencia Community College; Scott Hewit, Rollins College; Tracy Hickman, Lake City Community College; Marliese Hogan, Nova Southeastern University; Jeffrey Kaplan, University of Central Florida; Robert Kizlik, Florida Atlantic University; Ruth Lowery, University of Florida; Rose Pringle, University of Florida; Linda Ray, Florida Gulf Coast University; and Nancy Williams, University of South Florida.
- Thanks to Sweta Desai for her research support and cheerful good nature.
- Thanks, finally, to Pam Flynn.

TEACHER PREP

**MERRILL
PRENTICE HALL**

Teacher Preparation Classroom

See a demo at
www.prenhall.com/teacherprep/demo

Your Class. Their Careers. Our Future. Will your students be prepared?

We invite you to explore our new, innovative and engaging website and all that it has to offer you, your course, and tomorrow's educators! Organized around the major courses pre-service teachers take, the Teacher Preparation site provides media, student/teacher artifacts, strategies, research articles, and other resources to equip your students with the quality tools needed to excel in their courses and prepare them for their first classroom.

This ultimate on-line education resource is available at no cost, when packaged with a Merrill text, and will provide you and your students access to:

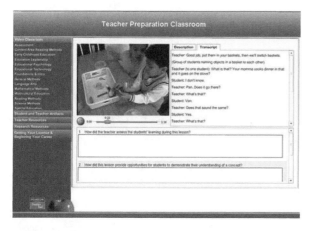

Online Video Library. More than 150 video clips—each tied to a course topic and framed by learning goals and Praxis-type questions—capture real teachers and students working in real classrooms, as well as in-depth interviews with both students and educators.

Student and Teacher Artifacts. More than 200 student and teacher classroom artifacts—each tied to a course topic and framed by learning goals and application questions—provide a wealth of materials and experiences to help make your study to become a professional teacher more concrete and hands-on.

Research Articles. Over 500 articles from ASCD's renowned journal *Educational Leadership.* The site also includes Research Navigator, a searchable database of additional educational journals.

Teaching Strategies. Over 500 strategies and lesson plans for you to use when you become a practicing professional.

Licensure and Career Tools. Resources devoted to helping you pass your licensure exam; learn standards, law, and public policies; plan a teaching portfolio; and succeed in your first year of teaching.

Brief Contents

Contents

Note: Every effort has been made to provide accurate and current Internet information in this book. However, the Internet and information posted on it are constantly changing, so it is inevitable that some of the Internet addresses listed in this textbook will change.

Introduction

Welcome to *Florida Standards: A Handbook for Teaching in the Sunshine State.* Perhaps you are wondering if teaching will be your profession; maybe you are already in a classroom and are confident that you have found your calling. You may have been asked to read this book as a supplemental course requirement; possibly, as a new teacher, you seek information.

As the author of the book, I can only imagine who my readers may be, but I have chosen to address myself primarily to you, the beginning teacher, in the hope that this book will be a tool, a link of sorts, between your beliefs about good teaching in general and what you may know about being a good teacher in a standards-based system of teaching and learning.

As you read this book, you may acquire some new factual knowledge; or some insight into your developing skills or specific strategies you can use in the classroom; or begin to feel more confident about yourself as a teacher. It is my hope that reading this book will inspire you to reconsider your beliefs, what you value in theory and in practice, and that you will continue to revisit your personal philosophy for teaching, especially as it connects to the results of your work.

I have framed the book in a standards-based model, addressing learning goals and objectives for attaining the desired outcomes. For each chapter, I have identified three goals, one from each domain of learning: knowledge (Figure 1), skill (Figure 2), and dispositions (Figure 3).

In terms of *declarative,* or factual, information, after reading this book you will know more about teaching and learning in a standards-based system, especially in Florida today.

Further, in terms of *procedural,* or skill, development, if you perform the activities presented in this book, you will also be creating and monitoring a professional development plan.

Finally, in terms of *affective,* or dispositional, development, as you reflect on the experiences you have while reading this book, your educational philosophy may undergo noticeable shifts.

Invitations to monitor your thinking about your own growth are located in boxes throughout each chapter. As a window into the complex issues addressed in this handbook, *Taking a Stance* offers position statements for you to consider. These statements appear at the beginning of each chapter, serving as an entrance point to the issues that follow. They are deliberately open-ended, residing more in opinion than fact.

Informing Your Stance and *Articulating Your Stance,* mid-chapter checkpoints, occur within each chapter. The questions they contain direct you to reconsider your initial thinking, reflect more deeply, and share your emerging opinions in discussions with colleagues.

Figure 1   Declarative goals and objectives.

After reading this book, you will:

I. Know more about teaching and learning in a standards-based system and be able to:

  1.1.1 Identify characteristics of effective teaching.

  1.1.2 Explain features of two accountability measures used in Florida: the Florida Teacher Certification Exam (FTCE) and the Florida Comprehensive Assessment Test (FCAT).

  2.1.1 Describe the connection between teaching and learning.

  2.1.2 Understand features of Florida's standards for teaching and learning: the *Florida Educator Accomplished Practices* (*FEAP*) and the *Sunshine State Standards.*

  3.1.1 Explain the process of planning.

  3.1.2 Differentiate between goals, objectives, and standards.

  4.1.1 Identify elements of standards-based lesson planning.

  4.1.2 Analyze features of lesson plan formats.

  5.1.1 Describe the role of reflection in the teaching-learning cycle.

  5.1.2 Explain methods of self-assessment.

  6.1.1 Define collaborative partnerships.

  6.1.2 Identify resources for teaching and learning.

After reading this book, you will be able to:

II. Monitor personal, professional development.

  1.2.1 Draft an initial professional development plan.

  1.2.2 Establish goals for meeting accountability challenges.

  2.2.1 Discuss a plan for passing the FTCE.

  2.2.2 Discuss ideas for preparing students to pass the FCAT.

  3.2.1 Write learning goals aligned with standards.

  3.3.2 Reflect on your methods for planning.

  4.2.1 Design detailed procedures for lessons.

  4.2.2 Design developmentally appropriate and interdisciplinary lessons.

  5.2.1 Plan methods for collecting and analyzing data.

  5.2.2 Draft a formal philosophy of education.

  6.2.1 Establish a network for personal, professional support.

  6.2.2 Craft new goals for ongoing professional development.

Figure 2   Procedural goals and objectives.

Figure 3 Dispositional goals and objectives.

After reading this book, you will be able to:

III. Refine personal philosophies for teaching and learning.

1.3.1 Understand the nature of assessment and accountability.

1.3.2 Analyze the role of teachers in impacting student learning.

2.3.1 Describe the nature of standards as a guide for teaching and learning.

2.3.2 Evaluate the content of standards in light of student needs.

3.3.1 Understand the importance of backward planning.

3.3.2 Appreciate the role of assessment to guide good instruction.

4.3.1 Relish the role of teachers as curriculum planners.

4.3.2 Synthesize components of effective teaching.

5.3.1 Revise earlier beliefs about teaching and learning.

5.3.2 Evaluate different models of lesson plans.

6.3.1 Collaborate with key stakeholders.

6.3.2 Advocate on behalf of all students.

To help you demonstrate mastery of the book's goals and objectives, each chapter summary concludes with questions aligned with the performance indicators established for each chapter. These questions are designed to demonstrate your thinking.

Researching Your Stance and *Extending Your Stance* suggest further explorations for your consideration—opportunities to think more critically, gather more data, and support your opinions with evidence. Extension activities are designed to expand and develop further insights at this stage of your teaching career. Much of the writing that you will complete as you interact with this handbook will document your emerging professionalism. When polished, your work will be suitable to use as artifacts in a professional portfolio.

I have chosen to use a rather informal style, adopting a more conversational tone—less the gray-haired professor and more the classroom teacher (and student)—because I would like to think that this book promotes open *discussion* about the nature and evolution of standards-based curricula. May you find it useful.

Chapter 1

The Teaching–Learning Connection

Goals and Objectives

After reading this chapter, readers will be able to:

I. Know more about teaching and learning in a standards-based system.
    1.1.1 Identify characteristics of effective teaching.
    1.1.2 Explain features of two accountability measures used in Florida: the Florida Teacher Competency Exam (FTCE) and the Florida Comprehensive Assessment Test (FCAT).

II. Monitor personal, professional development.
    1.2.1 Draft an initial professional development plan.
    1.2.2 Establish goals for meeting accountability challenges.

III. Refine personal philosophies for teaching and learning.
    1.3.1 Understand the nature of assessment and accountability.
    1.3.2 Analyze the role of teachers in influencing student learning.

This chapter is a general discussion about the impact of teachers on student learning and an introduction to the accountability demands faced by teachers as well as students. Two of Florida's standardized tests are explained.

To think before reading about some of the issues discussed in this chapter, consider the statements in Taking a Stance. Take a few minutes to jot down your thoughts. Be sure to offer reasons and examples to explain your feelings.

Perhaps as you thought about your own beliefs concerning the ideas in Taking a Stance you found yourself strongly agreeing or disagreeing. Certainly, each of these statements is

---

TAKING A STANCE

To what extent do you agree or disagree with the following statements?

1. Holding teachers accountable for student learning is a bad idea and should not be done.
2. The job of the teacher is to provide good instruction; the rest is up to students.
3. Teachers can and should be held accountable for student learning.

---

open to debate. Declarations made out of context can rarely be considered absolute truths, and different readers have different perspectives. If you are reading this book with others, discuss your feelings. Where do you stand? Why do you believe what you do? Under what conditions do these statements hold true, or not, for you?

Read this first chapter with an open mind. Because beliefs are shaped by experience, cultural norms, and social conventions, values can change with time and place. In the discussion that follows, I include my own ideas, providing a glimpse into one teacher's worldview, as well as the expressed views of the profession, situated in current policy and debate. I also include the thoughts of various educators currently teaching in the Sunshine State.

As you read and talk with others, reconsider your initial reflections. Perhaps you may notice some shifts in the opinions you expressed before reading, thinking, and sharing. Also, if you take time during your reading to reflect more deeply on your beliefs, your initial ideas will become stronger and better informed.

Teachers Who Make a Difference

When I was in fourth grade, my family moved from Idaho Falls, Idaho, to Lucas Valley, California, and I discovered the magic of the ice plant. If I broke a piece of this finger-shaped ground cover from the main plant, a thick, succulent juice flowed abundantly. If I used the juice as a medium for writing, it produced invisible text that emerged as a brown script only when exposed to light.

One Sunday afternoon, after the sun had moved behind the hills of the town, with absorbed fascination I wrote in invisible ice plant all over Lucas Valley Elementary School. I don't remember what I said, but I do remember using my formidable skill in cursive writing and said several walls-full, all in silent succulent.

About noon the next day, the principal hauled me out of class with a bucket of soapy water and a huge scrub brush. It was within the view of my classroom window that, no Tom Sawyer, I washed the entire school single-handedly.

The following afternoon Ms. McKenzie, my big-hearted fourth-grade teacher, called me to her desk during a quiet writing time. I knew I was in trouble again.

"Susan," she whispered sternly, "when you grow up, you must go to college and major in English."

And so I did. Later, I became a teacher of English language arts who wished to inspire my own students, much as Ms. McKenzie had influenced me.

What does it mean to be a good teacher, a teacher who makes a difference? Ms. McKenzie was a teacher who made a difference in my life for reasons beyond the ice plant. For one thing, she was the first teacher to publish my writing, a short poem about a bird. It perched for months on the classroom bulletin board, only to be replaced by a story I wrote about how Rebecca Revere, daughter of Paul Revere, witnessed the Battle of Concord by hiding under a shrub. Ms. McKenzie was also the first teacher to hook me on reading. I still remember crying about Jody, the main character, while Ms. McKenzie read to us from Marjorie Kinnan Rawlings' *The Yearling,* a beautiful story set in Florida, a magical place I hoped one day to visit.

Actually, Ms. McKenzie was the first teacher I remember. The difference she made in my life is profound on many levels, due largely to the fact that she was the first teacher to single me out. Because my family moved often—by age 18, I had lived in 18 different houses in seven states and two countries—I was usually the new kid, arriving on a Wednesday afternoon in the middle of a school year. Assigned to a seat in the back of the room, I was largely ignored by most of my teachers, who were probably too busy with their established students and who were still awaiting my school records from the last town in which I lived, records that rarely arrived before our next move. Unlike other teachers, Ms. McKenzie put me in the front row and paid attention. She took time to get to know me. She discovered that I was a reader, and she encouraged me to be a writer as well. She cared.

Think about your own experiences with effective teachers and take time to inform your stance about teaching effectiveness (see Informing Your Stance). As you recall what mattered to you as a student, continue to reflect on your own beliefs as a teacher and to share your opinions with colleagues. As you discuss the features of effective teaching with others, listen carefully to the perspectives of those whose opinions differ.

What Makes an Effective Teacher?

Describing the features of effective teaching is difficult due to variations in perspective, time, and context. Do you remember the story of the blind men and the elephant? Ed Young retells it beautifully in *Seven Blind Mice* (2002). In his version, one mouse runs up

---

❙NFORMING YOUR STANCE

1. What teachers made a difference in your life? Whether you remember a teacher from the time when you were very young or someone who specialized in physical education, botany, or art, consider the good teacher who made a positive contribution.
2. Why were these teachers remarkable? What special qualities did they have? What kinds of things did they do? What do you think they believed about teaching?

the elephant's tail and is certain he is on a rope. Another one, on the ear, believes the elephant must be a fan. As the perspective shifts, readers understand how vantage point defines the world.

Different participants in the education process may view effectiveness differently. Students, for example, may define an effective teacher as one who is "friendly, easy to get along with, and doesn't yell at you" (Batten, Marland, & Khamis, 1993), whereas for parents, an effective teacher is one who inspires students to work outside of school or gives appropriate homework assignments (Epstein, in Stronge & Ostrander, 1997). Principals concerned with issues of behavior may cite the number of referrals to demonstrate a teacher's effectiveness. An experienced high school teacher may point to expertise in a content area, whereas a beginning teacher, still a bit insecure, may judge her own effectiveness by her popularity with students.

Heraclitis said that we never step in the same river twice. Time, ever fluid, may also determine the degree of a teacher's effectiveness. To principals making observations, teachers at the *end* of a school year may appear more effective than at the *start* of a new year, just as a veteran teacher may draw on years of experience and grow stronger as a result.

Perceptions change in retrospect. For example, how many of your recollections about the teachers who made a difference in your own life included teachers who *at the time* seemed a bit unreasonable? I had to become an educator before fully appreciating the talents of my own teachers. Hindsight is often 20/20.

If you asked students in my university classroom about my effectiveness as a teacher, their answers would depend on their level of cognitive dissonance. At midterm, stressed about pending deadlines, students may complain about the workload, perhaps doubting the quality of my teaching, but by the end of the semester, if the work reaches logical fruition and leads to meaningful accomplishment, the same students may give my teaching high marks.

Context also changes everything (Bickmore, Smagorinsky, & O'Donnell-Allen, 2005). If you have spent time in any classroom as a teacher, you have discovered that what works for the same children one day may fail the next, or that a brilliant lesson taught first period may fall flat during fourth. A highly effective secondary teacher may be a dismal failure in second grade, while an award-winning math teacher may have no ability to teach anything else. Student teachers who soar during an internship sometimes find themselves struggling as first-year teachers when placed in a very different school culture. Teaching in Miami is vastly different from teaching in Chattahochee, and methods that work in Tallahassee's North-side schools may not work at all in the South side.

Simply stated, schools vary and so do children. The fact that teachers succeed once is no guarantee that they will again. Every learning experience is a new challenge, and effectiveness is related to myriad factors that shift with time, perspective, culture, and conditions. Teachers must work hard to be successful in each situation.

Our society expects teachers to be effective (Darling-Hammond & Youngs, 2002). Teachers are hired for one reason—to teach so that all students learn. Ideally, all parents want effective teachers for their children; all principals seek effective teachers for their school teams; and all teachers work extremely hard, to the best of their ability, in all kinds of conditions in order to serve their students, parents, and administrators.

According to Tameka King, a high school English teacher for 6 years, "When I first started teaching, I thought an effective teacher was the teacher who could get every student to learn. Now I believe that an effective teacher is the teacher who can get students to *want* to learn. An effective teacher is the teacher who can get students to be excited about whatever it is that excites them even if it isn't subject/verb agreement. Effective teachers stir parts of students' hearts and awaken minds dulled by the lull of routine education. When students walk out of the classroom still thinking, still processing a lesson even though final projects have been turned in and tests taken, the teacher has been effective."[*]

Julie Langston, a veteran middle school teacher, agrees. "When I began teaching, I initially thought an effective teacher was one who had total class control," she said. "Since then, I've learned that a good teacher is one who gives students control and yet still maintains order and discipline within the classroom."[†]

So, in a deeply complex process, teachers who make a difference do many things well. In large part, effective teaching requires certain attitudes, or dispositions, as well as knowledge and skill. The research on teaching effectiveness is clear (Marzano, 2003; Stronge, Tucker, & Hindman, 2004). Effective teachers *care* deeply and like young people. They are passionately enthusiastic and optimistic. They have a sense of humor. They are hardworking. They are sensitive to issues of diversity. They have excellent communication and interpersonal skills. They see their subject matter everywhere. They learn with their students. They advocate on behalf of all students, and they are knowledgeable about curriculum design, assessment, and good instruction. As you work closely with strong mentors and develop into a top-notch teacher yourself, you will continue to ponder issues of effectiveness as you continue to make a difference.

Consider These Beliefs

This book embodies the following principles: Teaching well is an art. Teachers who truly make a difference in the lives of students are passionate about their work. In the service of education, such teachers are dedicated to their mission: helping all students learn. Ultimately, they are optimists, having faith that even the most disengaged, disruptive, or disabled learner will grow—stronger, happier, and more skilled—given enough time and support. *Such teachers believe that they themselves are the ones most responsible for what their students learn, and these teachers utilize every resource to reach their goals.*

Teaching well, as I often tell my students who aspire to be teachers, is possibly the hardest job on the planet, and developing a passion for teaching requires personal and professional beliefs that cannot necessarily be taught but can be examined through self-reflection. As one teacher confided, "I do not know that I am a good teacher. I know that

---

[*]By permission from Tameka King.
[†]By permission from Julie Langston.

1. Consider your professional goals. Where do you hope to be 5 years from now? Imagine yourself as a classroom teacher and describe the nature of the work you will be doing.
2. Hopefully, your aim is to teach in the classroom you imagine. Assume that this is true and explain what you will do to ensure that you are effective.
3. Imagine the support systems you will have as a classroom teacher. How will you be sure that you thrive and not merely survive?

I am a good person who wants to be a good teacher. I know that my students are constantly on my mind; I am always thinking of ways to do what I did better the next time."

The demands on teachers are incredibly heavy, and even the most patient and enthusiastic teacher fails to leap out of bed *every* morning eager to get to school. Some days, even the best educators consider an alternative career, knowing, for example, that the same skills that work in a classroom are likely to elicit success selling used cars, pharmaceuticals, insurance, or Tupperware! For those who love this profession, such moments, though not uncommon, are usually translated into jokes shared with colleagues—other teachers like themselves who continue to get up every morning and go to school, tirelessly working with their students and finding the inner resources to *thrive*, not merely survive.

In the face of great challenges, passionate teachers continue to learn all they can about how to do their work better. Teacher Julie Langston admits, "If something doesn't work, I look for ways to fix it. My students talk to me and give me feedback because I ask for it regularly and they know I respect them."[‡]

Veteran teacher Tameka King remains passionate. "I still feel like every day is my first day of teaching," she explains, "not because I am not prepared or lack confidence, but because I never want to feel that I am not still learning."[§]

Passionate teachers sustain their professional identities. They join professional organizations, read educator journals, and seek help from outside. They love what they do. They accept and believe that student success rests in their hands, and in moments of grave doubt they keep students in their hearts.

Reflect on your plans to be an effective teacher (Informing Your Stance) and take time to inform your stance, discussing your intentions with others who value teaching as a lifelong career.

The Ultimate Accountability

In the rhetoric of national education reform, definitions of teacher effectiveness have narrowed. In the current climate of **accountability** (Reeves, 2004; Resnick & Zurawsky, 2005), school success is determined almost solely in terms of student achievement, as

[‡]By permission from Julie Langston.
[§]By permission from Tameka King.

more than ever before, teacher competency is being interpreted to include not only the demonstration of the teacher's knowledge, skills, and dispositions, but also the teacher's ability to impact K–12 student learning (NCATE, 1999). Accrediting agencies and government legislation are mandating standards, curriculum, and assessment (Lashway, 1999), and school reform efforts have evolved from a focus on curriculum and standards to an expectation of results (Walberg, 2003).

Since the Elementary and Secondary Education Act (ESEA) was enacted in 1965, the federal government has increased its role in public education. The main goals of the ESEA were to set high standards for learning, establish an accountability system, and articulate the conviction that all children can learn, regardless of their ability or background. To address its primary aim of influencing student learning through a long-term, broad-based effort, *The Goals 2000: Educate America Act,* established in 1994 and amended in 1996, has resulted in a major emphasis on teachers, and teachers have become the stakeholders most responsible for the demonstrated knowledge of their students (Holdzkom, 1999).

More recently, the No Child Left Behind Act (NCLB, 2001), signed into law by president George W. Bush in 2002 and virtually renaming ESEA, proposed to increase accountability for student growth in reading as well as other areas of education. As a condition for receiving federal education funds, NCLB requires states to do two important things: (a) establish a set of goals for educational improvement and (b) administer state-designed tests to measure performance toward those goals. The controversial and largely unpopular NCLB (Dykema, 2002; Yinger, 2005) radically increased the federal government's role in K–12 education, with devastating consequences for teachers and students alike (McElroy, 2005; Swaim, 2005).

Like it or not, agree or disagree, teachers are increasingly expected to assume responsibility for student progress in learning (Cochran-Smith, 2005; Reeves, 2004). As a result, teacher education programs are adjusting to the increased demand to prepare teachers who can achieve high levels of student learning (Cawelti, 1995; Cochran-Smith, 2003; Cohen, 1995; Dangel & Guyton, 2005; Darling-Hammond, 1996; Eisner, 1998).

In past decades, teachers were deemed effective and thereby certified to teach in the public schools if they attended a licensed teacher education program, passed a licensure examination, and completed a field experience. In the old model of teacher training, competencies other than student learning were stressed. Lesson planning, for example, was a major emphasis, and novice teachers were judged on their written lesson and unit plans. During a final field experience, beginning teachers were observed teaching and were judged on their ability to implement their plans; supervisors looked for demonstrated proficiency in skills such as organization, time management, and classroom management (Anderson, 1991; Beerens, 2000; Stronge, 1997).

In my own preparation to become a teacher, major points were awarded for designing interactive bulletin boards and for developing my own ability to model cursive writing (a skill mastered, you may recall, under the guidance of Ms. McKenzie). We took entire courses on how to use the overhead and slide projectors and practiced threading 18 mm film through the machine. Some things have clearly changed!

Even in recent books for teachers, the secrets of successful teaching still include making friends with building personnel, organizing the classroom, setting rules, managing paperwork, motivating students, building good relationships with parents, networking with professionals, and so on (Creemers, 1994; Kottler, Kottler, & Kottler, 1998; Stronge 2002). Such aims certainly typify the professional educator and describe the context of the teacher's work, but accountability for *student learning* is glaringly absent. Today, by contrast, the main criterion for successful teaching—no secret in any school district and a major aim of Florida's system of school grading—is the teacher's ability to foster high levels of learning (Darling-Hammond, 1999).

The old model of teacher training now seems inadequate. Systematic school accountability requires teacher education programs to prepare teachers who can foster high levels of learning in students (Cochran-Smith, 2005; Kanstoroom & Finn, 1999; Lunenberg & Korthagen, 2003).

Increased accountability demands not only affect K–12 schools and classroom teachers; more than ever, colleges of education are expected to scrutinize, and document, how well their graduates achieve the state and national standards (NCATE, 1999).

The National Council for Accreditation of Teacher Education (NCATE) 2000 standards have added student learning as a critical feature, the bottom line in just about every standard. In the language of NCATE, preservice teachers are referred to as *candidates,* and teacher education programs are revising their efforts to better support candidates as they strive to connect their teaching to the learning of their students.

In line with national reform, the new model of teacher education, as demonstrated in programs adjusting to the new accountability, is often based on several key features, such as more time spent in actual classrooms, multiple assessment strategies, problem-based learning, performance assessment, and peer and self-assessment (Heywood, 2000; Rankin, 1999).

In the changing world of teacher preparation, alternative pathways for licensure are encouraged (Cochran-Smith, 2005; Simmons, 2005), as long as the prospective teacher meets the standards. To address the increasingly critical need for teachers, in the state of Florida teachers attain certification via many routes: traditional teacher education degrees, alternative certification, a model of state professional preparation, and the recent Educator Preparation Institute model. The American Board for Certification has contracted with Florida to offer a Passport to Teaching program. The decisive standard for all candidates, regardless of the route to licensure, is that educators must be able to foster high levels of learning in the students they teach. Student learning has become everybody's business.

Connecting Teaching and Learning

Connecting teaching and learning is certainly not a new idea. The best teachers, those whom we credit with making a difference, have always been effective in achieving results, and the best teacher education programs continually seek methods for increased effectiveness. Stakes now are higher than in the past; we must all strengthen the relationship between the standards guiding what teachers teach, the methods teachers use, and what students learn (Wiggins, 1996).

Teachers interested in fostering a clearer connection between the plans they make, the lessons they teach, and, ultimately, the gains their students make face a three-pronged challenge: (a) how to target *appropriate* standards, thereby determining what they want students to learn; (b) how to design lessons that result in high levels of student learning; (c) and, in the end, how to demonstrate—to students, parents, principals, other interested participants, and themselves—that they made a difference in the learning, and lives, of all students, including those with learning disabilities, language barriers, and other special needs.

Teaching is a human endeavor. Increasingly, teachers must confront the overwhelming needs of students: students dropping out of school in large numbers, students struggling to understand a second language, and poor students marginalized by society. To understand the multifaceted challenges testing their students, teachers must be "intelligent, sensitive, caring, and demanding individuals" (Moulthrop, Calegarl, & Eggers, 2005, p. 284).

The art of teaching is complex, and today's educators need sophisticated skills (Wayne & Youngs, 2003). Good assessment, the lens through which to understand the teaching and learning processes, has become an essential tool for meeting the challenge of standards-based instruction.

Assessment and Accountability

In a **standards-based educational system**, an effort-dependent view of schooling (Resnick & Klopfer, 1996), teachers set high standards designed to garner higher levels of student effort, and the results are monitored in order to judge the quality of student work, as well as to guide further instruction. Well-designed standards are essential since they serve as the blueprint for the construction of learning, the road map for the educational journey. *Without attention to instruction, the development and use of high standards has little or no correlation to high outcomes.* In other words, although standards help codify what is expected, they do not necessarily result in student learning. Instead, a focus on assessment and accountability requires educators to rethink their instructional program.

In theory, accountability improves teacher effectiveness because it obligates teachers to determine whether they are achieving their goals and to adjust their instruction accordingly (Blackwell, 1997; Lashway, 1999; Wiggins, 1996). Aligning standards with outcomes takes significant time and energy, and educators at all levels are grappling with ways to transform the teaching/learning process in order to meet the standards that govern and so ensure success on competency assessments (Mentkowski, 2000).

Competency, or achievement, testing is not new, and it has always been widespread. Think of a career—lawyer, hair dresser, doctor, soldier, or teacher. Just about any field, any endeavor, involves a test. Attorneys must pass the bar exam, and cosmetologists must pass state board exams. Medicine requires numerous tests of competency, and the military determines rank according to scores earned on aptitude tests. Acronyms like SRUSS, CTBS, ACT, SAT, CLAST, NAEP, HSCT, and GRE are probably familiar to American students.

Even as a student in Ms. McKenzie's fourth-grade class, I recall learning how to fill in circles, making my marks heavy and dark, and completely erasing any marks I did not want. And when I turned 16, applying for my first job at Sears, I was asked to take a test that determined whether I would be allowed to work a cash register. Like most persons reading this book, I took the Scholastic Aptitude Test (SAT) to enter college and the Graduate Record Exam (GRE) to continue my education. When I applied for my teaching license in Kentucky, I first had to pass a state exam.

So, why do notions of accountability, currently the subject of great debate, seem far more important today? For one thing, in the 1970s and 1980s, newspapers began to publish test scores and thereby to publicly rank schools according to the results (Popham, 1999). Ever since then, the issue of student achievement has grown in direct proportion to the public's awareness, informed by a single standardized test score. Not only do families now buy and sell houses based on the quality of local schools, but teachers have a justifiable reason to "teach to the test."

Accountability, a critical issue for all citizens, is especially pertinent for teachers, for teacher candidates, and for students (Reeves, 2004). National professional organizations have been developing assessments to test teacher learning. For example, the Interstate New Teacher Assessment and Support Consortium (INTASC) has created the Test for Teaching Knowledge to measure declarative knowledge and skill, and the model INTASC portfolio serves as a standards-based performance assessment. INTASC recommends that teachers be tested in at least three ways, according to (a) a test of content knowledge, such as math or science; (b) a test of teaching knowledge and pedagogy; and (c) an assessment of actual teaching. Individual states are responsible for determining their own method of assessment.

Florida Assessments of Teaching and Learning

To discuss standards and accountability for teacher and student learning in more helpful terms, consider the state of Florida. The Florida Statewide Assessment Program, designed to assess students' academic strengths and weaknesses in basic skills, was formally established as an accountability system for the public schools in 1971. Since then, the Florida legislature has been a visible force authorizing and expanding a statewide testing program (Fisher, 1986). Currently, the Office of K–20 Education Information and Accountability (EIA) coordinates the statewide development of accountability measures, standards, and other attempts to improve educational performance.

Teachers and students are *both* required to demonstrate knowledge, skill, and dispositions as part of a program of accountability. Standards vary, but the concept of accountability applies across the board. Teachers must demonstrate mastery of the *Florida Educator Accomplished Practices (FEAP),* and students in Grades 3 to 12 must demonstrate mastery of the *Sunshine State Standards.* Both of these standards are discussed more fully in Chapter 2.

To determine competency, teachers and students are both tested. In order to be certified to teach in Florida and to demonstrate mastery of teaching standards, teacher candidates must pass the Florida Teacher Certification Exam (FTCE). In order to graduate from Florida's schools and to demonstrate mastery of learning standards, students must pass the Florida Comprehensive Assessment Test (FCAT).

Florida Teacher Certification Exam (FTCE)

The **Florida Teacher Certification Exam (FTCE)** is mandated by the Florida legislature for *all* teacher candidates seeking certification. Candidates must demonstrate mastery of basic skills, professional knowledge, and knowledge in their content area of specialization. Testing requirements for teacher candidates seeking certification are described in Section 1012.56, Florida Statutes (FS), and in 6A-4.0021, Florida Administrative Code (FAC).

Currently, most candidates take three tests as part of the FTCE: (a) the General Knowledge Test, (b) the Professional Education Test, and (c) the Subject Area Exam. The General Knowledge Test, a basic skills achievement test, contains three multiple-choice sections—with about 40 items in mathematics, reading, and English language skills—and a written essay section. This test is usually administered in the morning. The Professional Education Test, also with a multiple-choice format, is designed to assess general knowledge of pedagogy and professional practices. It consists of approximately 120 items and is usually administered in the afternoon.

In addition to the General Knowledge and Professional Education Tests, candidates must pass a subject area exam in the field in which they are seeking certification. This exam measures content area knowledge, usually in a multiple-choice format, and the number of items varies from approximately 80 to 140, depending on the subject area. English 6–12, Middle Grades English 5–9, French K–12, German K–12, and Spanish K–12 also require an essay. Spanish K–12 and French K–12 have a speaking component and are administered in a language lab, and German K–12 includes a tape-recorded interview. Speech 6–12 includes a videotaped portion.

To assist with preparation for the FTCE, *Competencies and Skills Required for Teacher Certification in Florida, Ninth Edition* is a publication produced by the Florida Department of Education that includes a comprehensive list of the state's requirements for demonstrating competency and knowledge in professional education, general knowledge, and the various subject areas. Test preparation guides are also available to help candidates prepare for the certification tests. More current information can be found on the Florida Department of Education Web site (*http://www.fldoe.org*).

The Bureau of Educator Certification at the Department of Education determines individualized testing requirements for certification. If you have a certification application on file, the Bureau will inform you of your individual testing requirements. The Bureau advises teacher candidates to submit an application for certification before applying to take certification examinations.

To apply for certification online, visit the Florida Department of Education Web site and click on Educator Certification or contact the Bureau of Educator Certification (toll free in Florida: 800-445-6739).

Florida Comprehensive Assessment Test (FCAT)

The **Florida Comprehensive Assessment Test (FCAT)** is a large-scale standardized test, mandated by the state legislature. It is designed to assess the achievement of Florida's students and is used for several purposes.

According to the Department of K–12 Assessment in the Florida Department of Education, the primary purpose of the FCAT is to assess student achievement of high-order thinking skills represented in the *Sunshine State Standards*. That portion of the FCAT is a **criterion-referenced test (CRT)**.

The secondary purpose of the FCAT is to compare the performance of Florida students to that of students from across the nation. This is done through the use of a **norm-referenced test (NRT)** for reading and mathematics. The current NRT is the Stanford Achievement Test 10 (SAT 10), published by Harcourt Assessment.

Basically, the four parts of the FCAT are given annually, during February and March, to all students in Grades 3 through 10. The first three portions of the exam are criterion-referenced, and, the first part measures student achievement in reading, writing, and mathematics. The second part, administered in Grades 4, 8, and 10, is an essay test on an assigned topic. The third part, given to students in Grades 5, 8, and 10, is a science test. The fourth part, the norm-referenced section, is used to compare the performance of Florida students in reading and math in Grades 3 through 10 to that of students from other states.

The development of the FCAT, from the design stage through review and scoring of individual test items, is done with input by Florida educators. The Department of Education convenes and facilitates over 70 different committees, comprised of over 600 Florida educators and citizens from nearly every county in the state. For example, content advisory committees meet to identify the reading, writing, science, and math benchmarks to be assessed. The Bias Review Committee, representing Florida's regional, racial/ethnic, and cultural diversity, reviews passages, prompts, and test items for potential bias. In addition to other committees, special ad hoc groups comprised of parents, teachers, school administrators, and others meet to review various aspects of the testing program and to advise the Department of Education on courses of action.

In spite of extensive efforts to ensure participation of all citizens, the FCAT has been a contentious subject for several reasons. Some argue that the test does not adequately assess student learning, nor does it provide data instructionally useful to classroom teachers (Kysilka, 2005; Popham, 2005). One issue, however, seems to dominate the public debates.

The stakes are high for students. This particular aspect of standardized testing in Florida has been especially controversial. Third graders, for example, who score low on the FCAT are not promoted to the next grade, and in order to graduate from high school, all students must pass the 10th-grade FCAT.

The stakes are also high for schools. In Florida, students are not the only ones to get grades and report cards. The state also gives every public school a letter grade. *The A+ Plan for Education* is an accountability system that identifies schools that do well and schools that need improvement.

FCAT scores are used to determine critically low-performing as well as high-performing schools (Wright, Barron, & Kromrey, 1999). Based on their overall performance on the FCAT (including the percentage of eligible students who took the test) and improvement gains by the lowest performing students, financial awards are distributed. School scores are also sent home to parents, published on "report cards" on the Florida Department of Education Web site, and publicized by the media. Students in failing schools can receive vouchers to attend another school, public or private.

ARTICULATING YOUR STANCE

1. What standardized tests have you taken thus far in your educational and professional careers?
2. In what ways have such tests helped you to succeed in your aims, and in what ways have they been problematic?
3. How will you prepare students for the FCAT?
4. How will you prepare yourself for the FTCE?

Consider what you know and believe about the role of standardized testing (Articulating Your Stance), and be sure to share your impressions with your colleagues.

A more detailed explanation of both the FCAT and the A+ Plan can be found on the Florida Department of Education's Web site. Other resources, including sample test books, are also available online (see Chapter 6).

SUMMARY >>

After reading this chapter, you now know more about teaching and learning in a standards-based system, especially the professional accountability of both teachers and students. You may be interested in reviewing your initial assumptions made at the start of this chapter (Taking a Stance). Notice any shifts in your assumptions.

In a final written reflection, as evidence that you have mastered the objectives of this chapter, take time to:

1. Describe the characteristics of effective teaching.
2. Explain the features of the FTCE.
3. Explain the features of the FCAT.
4. Write five or more personal goals related to your ongoing professional development. What do you need to accomplish, and how do you plan to do so?
5. As a key artifact for your professional portfolio, draft a brief statement outlining your personal philosophy about teaching and learning. Be sure to include the role of the teacher in influencing student learning, as well as the relationship between assessment and accountability.

PREAMBLE TO CONTINUED READING >>

Extending Your Stance offers suggestions for activities that will deepen your reflection about the connection between teaching and learning in our current age of accountability.

Keep in mind that the intent of this book is to push beyond discussions about higher tests scores, merit pay for teachers, programmatic hoop-jumping, or the advantages and

EXTENDING YOUR STANCE

1. Interview a classroom teacher. You might ask:
   - What requirements did you meet in order to be certified to teach?
   - How do you know you are a good teacher?
   - How has your understanding of what it means to be an effective teacher changed?
   - How might an outsider to your classroom know that you are passionate about your job?
   - In what ways, if any, have you made peace with FCAT testing?

2. If you can locate principals or other school administrators who are available for an interview, ask them to describe the features of teaching effectiveness.

3. Compare the answers you get with those of other interviewers. What patterns emerge? For example, in the responses of teachers, in what ways, if any, does length of experience matter?

4. Use the Internet to research another state. What requirements guide licensure there? What assessments determine teacher competency?

disadvantages of standardized tests like the FCAT or the FTCE. Instead, continue to think about your role as an effective teacher.

Research on teaching effectiveness (Marzano, 2003) reports that individual teachers have the power to make a strong impact on student learning. The best teachers employ "effective instructional strategies, classroom management techniques, and classroom curricular design in a fluent, seamless fashion" (Marzano, 2003, p. 77).

Consider these key points as a preamble for reading Chapter 2.

- As our educational system adjusts to a standards-based model of individualized instruction and increased accountability, and as the standards that guide teachers adjust as well, good teachers continue to do exactly what they have always done.
- Because teachers care about their students and because they are committed to helping all students, they continue to work hard. They are passionate even in the face of difficulty and disheartening political decisions.
- Effective teachers assume responsibility for student learning, and they envision and embrace models for teaching that work well with all learners.
- Mastery of tasks require that teachers articulate clear outcomes, choose appropriate tools, and incorporate effective strategies.
- The issues are complex, the work is not easy, and formidable barriers exist.

In Chapter 2, you will learn more about standards-based education. By understanding the history of national standards and the standards that currently guide teaching and learning in the Sunshine State, you will be better prepared to teach in a Florida classroom.

Standards-Based Learning

Goals and Objectives

After reading this chapter, readers will be able to:

I. Know more about teaching and learning in a standards-based system.
   2.1.1 Describe the connection between teaching and learning.
   2.1.2 Understand features of Florida's standards for teaching and learning: the *Florida Educator Accomplished Practices* and the *Sunshine State Standards*.

II. Monitor personal, professional development.
   2.2.1 Discuss a plan for passing the FTCE.
   2.2.2 Discuss ideas for preparing students to pass the FCAT.

III. Refine personal philosophies for teaching and learning.
   2.3.1 Describe the nature of standards as a guide for teaching and learning.
   2.3.2 Evaluate the content of standards in light of student needs.

In this chapter, standards-based learning is defined conceptually and historically. The national standards that govern teacher development and those that guide student learning are identified, and Florida's standards for both teachers and students are highlighted.

What does student learning look like, and who decides what students learn? What is the relationship between student learning and standards? *Standards* is a buzz word in the field of education. Undoubtedly, you have heard it before. As you consider the connotations and possible uses for *standards* (Taking a Stance) make some quick notes about your assumptions before reading this chapter.

To what degree do you agree or disagree with the following statements?

1. Student learning is the end result of effective teaching.
2. Standards get in the way of learning and limit what can be taught.
3. Teachers determine what students learn.

A Call to Standards-Based Learning

In many ways, nothing is different in a standards-based classroom. Teachers still do many things: they plan units and lessons, collect materials, prepare handouts, manage student behavior, determine class procedures, and maintain careful records, for instance. However, one thing is very different in a standards-based classroom. Instead of focusing on *teaching,* teachers who effectively foster student growth focus on *learning.* In such classrooms, learning is central—the point of every teaching endeavor.

The shift in emphasis from teaching to learning is often illustrated with a joke: Two men are sitting on the porch, and one says to the other, "Did I tell you that last week I taught my dog how to whistle?"

The buddy looks at the dog, sleeping silently nearby, and asks, "Why haven't I heard him whistling?"

The first man laughs, slaps his knee, and explains, "I said I *taught* him; I didn't say he learned it!"

In a standards-based classroom, when the emphasis of teaching is on learning, teachers *think* differently. As standards-based teachers plan lessons, collect materials, prepare handouts, and so on, their efforts are targeted to clearly articulated outcomes monitored to gauge their effect. Teachers think less about what *they* will do and more about what *students* will accomplish, focusing on methods and modifications for helping all students learn. Such teachers use formal and informal assessment, aligned to their aims and methods, and they adjust their teaching accordingly.

A Conceptual Model

To conceptualize a standards-based model, consider the qualities that make a good teacher. Instead of crediting teachers for being compassionate or organized, smart about their subjects, or people who grade fairly, the model expands to evaluate the *results* of such traits. Instead of thinking about the outcomes that demonstrate the teacher's knowledge or the application of that knowledge in a classroom setting, the model documents the *results* of the teacher's work. Various graphics could represent this shift.

Figure 2.1 depicts an expanded view of teaching effectiveness encompassing three aspects: (a) the teacher's knowledge, (b) the teacher's skill, or use of the teacher's knowledge in practice, and (c) the results or outcome of the teacher's abilities on student learning.

Figure 2.1 A model of teacher effectiveness.

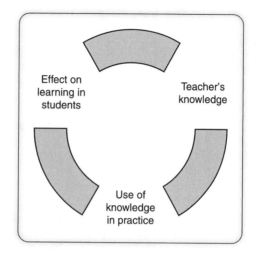

This conceptual model assumes that teacher dispositions are part of knowledge, skill, and effect. The model also suggests a process. Enter the cycle at any one of the three points and the others follow. The teacher's knowledge of teaching leads to the ability to implement that knowledge in a classroom, which impacts student learning. The effect on student learning informs the teacher and results in adjustments in practice.

In another representation of standards-based instruction, in a flowchart, for example, the many roles and responsibilities of a teacher lead eventually to a single outcome: the evaluation of student learning and the results of teaching (Figure 2.2). In this model of a cyclic process, teachers pay attention to student needs and what students know before they teach; then they target learning outcomes, planning and assessing accordingly.

Demonstrating that the end result of the teaching process is a difference in student learning can be done in a simple graphic as well. For example, in an inverted pyramid,

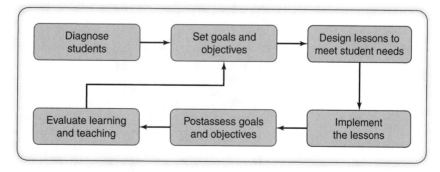

Figure 2.2 Flowchart of outcome evaluation.

Figure 2.3 The ultimate AP.

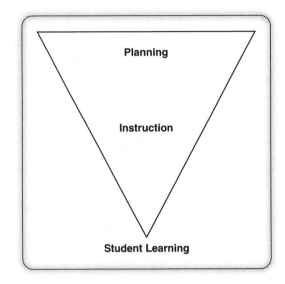

student learning becomes the point (Figure 2.3). Here, all decisions about planning and instruction are intended to lead to one thing: learning gains. These gains are the target, the ultimate accomplished practice.

In a model of standards-based learning consisting of a series of concentric circles, student learning is embedded at the core (Figure 2.4). All state, national, and local standards

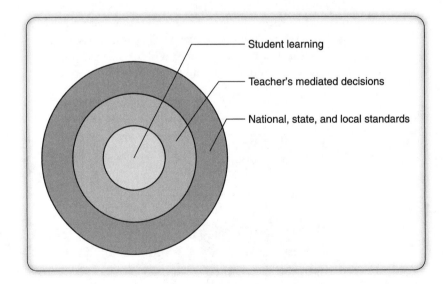

Figure 2.4 Standards as mediated by the teacher.

established to guide learning surround the planning decisions made by the teacher. Methods, materials, and assessments—all aspects of a teacher's curricular choices—serve to bridge the distance between the standards and the results. The teacher is the decisive element, the filter through which standards are interpreted. The results of the teacher's work are made visible in the evidence of student learning.

In Chapter 1, I argued that if the main goal of teaching is to promote student learning, and as student learning is increasingly scrutinized to demonstrate a teacher's effectiveness, then teachers need to adjust to this ultimate standard. As a classroom teacher, your philosophy of education will guide your every decision. Let your stance be one that assumes responsibility for every student's accomplishments, a vision that focuses on results. (Informing Your Stance). Such a vision is one of genuine caring, one that means you can take pride in the results of your work, knowing you have made a difference, and thus *enjoy* a career in the world's most rewarding profession.

If student learning is the ultimate outcome of teaching, then how a teacher defines *learning* is crucial.

Defining Learning

Because a standards-based curriculum focuses on student learning, the word *learning* has become prominent in the jargon of education. Semantically, *learning* has three applications, depending on the context in which it appears. Primarily, *learning* is a noun, naming a result or product: *Teachers communicate high expectations for <u>learning</u>. Learning* has a verb form too, referring to something being done, an experience, or a process: *Teachers are <u>learning</u> with their students. Learning* can also be used as an adjective, a description of something else: *Teachers create a <u>learning</u> environment.*

According to the *Encyclopaedia Britannica,* learning is the "process of acquiring modifications in existing knowledge, skills, habits, or tendencies through experience, practice, or exercise." For the most part, *learning* is an abstraction, a concept or idea, meaning different things to different people. How educators define the term tends to relate to one of two philosophical approaches. In one, as typified by the work of Robert Thorndike, son of

E. L. Thorndike, learning is an outcome, a set of measurable objectives, quantified and controlled. In the other, as described in the work of John Dewey, learning is a qualitatively complex process, experiential, creative, and personally compelling (Sarason, 2004).

The Thorndikes were psychologists who studied animal behavior and then applied the same principles to humans. Their research concerning stimulus-response theories and measurable outcomes has been foundational in theories related to behaviorism. Dewey, on the other hand, was an educator and philosopher who advocated for a more pragmatic, context-dependent view of human behavior as the result of knowledge and reasoning.

Whether learning is viewed as behaviors learned by association, as in stimulus-response contexts, or as insights individually constructed over time, the role of the teacher is crucial. Learning does not happen in a vacuum; it follows other types of learning. Think of a newborn baby, the original blank slate. As parents, the child's first teachers, and other adults model, guide, and encourage, the baby develops language (Bissex, 1980; Britton, 1982; Smith, 1998; Vygotsky, 1978).

Recent research (De Kock, Sleegers, & Voeten, 2004) defines *new learning* as learning that shifts from transmitted behaviors to knowledge construction and includes attention to affective skills, the learning process, the relationships between teachers and learners, and the relationships of learners to each other.

Undoubtedly, learning is a social phenomenon, inspired by the lives, the work, and the leadership of those who have come before us. Etymologically, *learning* derives from an Old English word, *last,* meaning "footprint," and a Latin word, *lira,* meaning a "furrow" or "track." Perhaps that is why learning is often described as a journey. The teacher's job is to make decisions about how best to help each student move further along the path (Articulating Your Stance).

National Standards for Teaching and Learning

If we can assume that learning is a journey, then **standards** represent the map, often handed to us by others. Standards attempt to specify outcomes, and they are written for different purposes (Ericsson, 2005). Standards for teacher education describe the desired learning to result from an educational program, and standards in public schools define the outcomes of formal education. Standards exist that identify what teachers should know and be able to do at different points in their careers, and different standards describe what students should know and be able to do at different points in their education.

Standards are most often written by committees of well-intended stakeholders. It is not unusual for practicing teachers, teacher educators, school leaders, parent representatives, business people, and state agency staff to work together. The process is intense and time-consuming. The committee usually begins with a thorough review of the mission of their organization, prior documentation, and the professional literature, using the best of what is known as a basis for crafting comprehensive standards. Before standards are approved, most organizations collect feedback and seek input from a broader constituency in order to revise and strengthen the committee's work.

Standards, because they are written by groups of people, vary, just as personal and collective philosophies vary. National professional organizations have each identified the declarative, procedural, and attitudinal knowledge they believe teachers as well as students need to have. Groups like the Interstate New Teacher Assessment and Support Consortium (INTASC), the National Board for Professional Teaching Standards (NBPTS), and the National Association of State Directors of Teacher Education and Certification (NASDTEC) have crafted generic standards for all teachers, while other groups such as the National Council of Teachers of Mathematics (NCTM), the National Association for the Education of Young Children (NAEYC), the American Alliance for Health, Physical Education, Recreation and Dance (AAHPERD), and the International Reading Association (IRA) have defined standards specific to professional areas of specialization for both teachers and students.

Standards can take different forms. Some of the standards for teacher learning, for example, are little more than a skills' checklist ("create a lesson plan") or a narrowly constructed test of knowledge ("list the levels of Bloom's taxonomy"). Others are more broadly conceptualized ("understand human development" or "incorporate technology as a tool for learning"). Standards can identify low-level learning ("define an objective") or require high-level application ("evaluate the features of good instruction"). In addition to knowledge and skills, some standards target the affective domain too ("believe that all students are learners," "value diversity," or "appreciate literature").

In times of shifting policies, political agendas, and educational reform, educators are easily frustrated both by the rapidity of change and by the issues still neglected in new mandates. Much has changed in teacher education, for instance, in the years since some of the current standards were adopted. Eventually, existing standards, as well as the need for new standards, change—just as student needs, classroom challenges, technological skills, societal demands, and other political realities change.

To date, many standards have yet to reflect the new accountability. For example, in addition to the NCATE 2000 standards, the Educational Testing Service (ETS) is one of the few sets of teacher education standards to make student learning a visible outcome. ETS standards address four domains of teaching, each focused directly on student learning. The language of these standards offers a model, potentially helpful, for guiding teacher education programs and teacher candidates toward student learning. The ETS domains include (a) organizing content knowledge for student learning, (b) creating an environment for student learning, (c) teaching for student learning, and (d) teacher professionalism. Even *professionalism* is described, for example, as the ability to reflect "on the extent to which the learning goals were met" (Danielson, 1996).

Professional organizations like the National Council of Teachers of English revise their teacher education guidelines every 10 years (NCTE, 1996). Many standards projects are adjusting to the rapid changes and current trends even as this book is written. The most recent versions of any standards are easily located on the Web.

Standards That Guide Teacher Learning

The professional development of teachers is guided by national and state standards, and a close look at the standards developed by different organizations will help you understand what is expected from you as a teacher. Since 1987, INTASC, a network of education organizations dedicated to the preparation of quality teachers, has been founded on the core principle that "an effective teacher must be able to integrate content knowledge with the specific strengths and needs of students to assure that *all* students learn and perform at high levels" (*http://www.ccsso.org/projects*). To support the belief that student learning is the cornerstone for all education policy, INTASC has established national *core standards* (1992) for what all beginning teachers should know, believe, and be able to do. INTASC is also establishing standards for content-specific disciplines like social studies and foreign language teaching, and has developed a series of assessments aligned with its standards.

Other national professional organizations have developed standards for what constitutes a professional educator in specific content areas. According to the standards written by NCTM, for example, teachers "use a variety of physical and visual materials for exploration and development of four basic operations with positive and negative rational numbers." Standards crafted by the Association for Childhood Education International (ACEI) direct teachers to "know the importance of establishing and maintaining a positive collaborative relationship with families to promote the intellectual, social, emotional, and physical growth of children."

States are also required to establish standards for quality teachers. Each state creates its own standards, and though states may call their standards something else, most rely on the INTASC standards, the National Council for Social Studies standards, and the standards of other national organizations as guides. The Teachers Standards and Practices Commission in Oregon has created the "TSPC Professional Standards for an Initial Teaching License"; the Oklahoma Commission for Teacher Preparation has drafted that state's "General Competencies for Licensure and Certification"; and the Vermont Standards Board for Professional Educators has developed "Five Standards for Vermont Educators" with corresponding indicators.

As you become familiar with the standards that define teacher learning, keep in mind that your own growth as a teacher is being guided by several sets of standards. To illustrate, my current position—teaching English in a Florida teacher education program—is informed by many different standards, including but not limited to national accreditation standards (NCATE), standards for teacher education (INTASC), standards for teaching secondary English (NCTE), standards for teaching reading (IRA), standards for teaching middle school (NMSA), Florida's standards for teacher education (*FEAP*), Florida's standards for student learning, (the *Sunshine State Standards*), and Florida's standards for teaching English language learners (ELL).

Just as state and national standards define the knowledge, skills, and dispositions required by teachers, other standards define what should be learned by K–12 students.

Standards That Guide Student Learning

What should children in second grade know and be able to do? What about students taking a high school science course? If a student takes algebra in California, is it taught the same way as in New York? **Content standards** define learning outcomes in academic subjects. **Benchmarks** define performances at various developmental or grade levels. And specific indicators or performance standards define discrete examples of more generalized knowledge and skill.

Few argue against educational standards, especially in light of equity issues. Standards are essential for schools desiring to offer a comprehensive, in-depth curriculum to all students. Prior to the advent of standards, "profound" differences existed, for example in high school courses taught in suburban versus urban or rural schools (French, 2003). Teachers at all levels understand that standards support meaningful teaching by providing a curricular framework for any subject at any grade level. As veteran high school teacher Carol Jago puts it, "Standards and standards-based materials can help teachers not have to make it up alone" (2002, p. 30).

Drawing on the national standards established by professional educational organizations, each state has developed standards for what its students should know and be able to do. Different state agencies determine their state's version of student standards, and though the names change with each state, the basic process is the same. The Texas Education Agency distributes the Texas Essential Knowledge and Skills (TEKS), Indiana's Accountability System for Academic Performance (ASAP) distributes Indiana's Academic Standards, the Georgia Office of Student Achievement (OSA) oversees the results of Georgia's Performance Standards, and in Florida the Bureau for School Performance guides educators on implementation of the *Sunshine State Standards*.

Florida Standards for Teaching and Learning

In the current system of educational policy, the aims of education are determined by adopted standards. Some sets of standards define learning outcomes for teacher development, and others mandate expectations for students. In Florida, teacher learning is guided by the *Florida Educator Accomplished Practices (FEAP), Competencies for Teachers of the Twenty-First Century,* and student learning is guided by the *Sunshine State Standards.* Teachers in Florida must demonstrate their mastery of the Accomplished Practices, and students in Florida must demonstrate their mastery of the *Sunshine State Standards.*

Florida Educator Accomplished Practices (FEAP)

Policies regarding teacher preparation are the jurisdiction of the Florida Education Standards Commission (ESC). Created in 1980, pursuant to Section 231.545, Florida Statutes, the Commission consists of 24 members, nominated by the Commissioner of Education, appointed by the State Board of Education, and confirmed by the Senate. Exactly half of the membership consists of classroom teachers, and all members of the ESC serve for 3-year staggered terms.

Duties and responsibilities of the ESC include approval of preservice teacher education programs; issues of teacher certification; evaluation of teaching competence; alternative ways to demonstrate qualifications for certification; and other policies regarding the professional development of educators. The Commission is also responsible for developing and implementing Florida's standards for teachers.

The **Florida Educator Accomplished Practices (FEAP)**, *Competencies for Teachers of the Twenty-First Century,* a generic set of teaching proficiencies, were developed by the ESC and adopted in 1996. Since that time, teacher educators in Florida have redesigned their teaching and testing practices in order to ensure that preservice teachers demonstrate the 12 preprofessional competencies (Figure 2.5). Program approval from the state is predicated on an institution's successful documentation of these standards, and teacher educators in programs across the state have become well versed in the *FEAPs*, targeting courses and designing sources of evidence to document candidate learning.

The 12 competencies are carefully worded to define, for the most part, what accomplished educators can do. In terms of assessment (Accomplished Practice #1 [AP #1]), for example, "The preprofessional teacher collects and uses data gathered from a variety of sources. These sources include both traditional and alternate assessment strategies. Furthermore, the teacher can identify and match the students' instructional plans with their cognitive, social, linguistic, cultural, emotional, and physical needs" (Florida Education Standards Commission, 1996).

1. Assessment
2. Communication
3. Continuous Improvement
4. Critical Thinking
5. Diversity
6. Ethics
7. Human Development and Learning
8. Knowledge of Subject Matter
9. Learning Environments
10. Planning
11. Role of the Teacher
12. Technology

Figure 2.5   The *FEAPs*.

To clarify and exemplify the demonstrated skills that evidence each *FEAP,* the Commission also drafted sample key indicators. For example, one sample performance offered to support assessment (AP #1) states that the preprofessional educator "guides students in maintaining individual portfolios." Such an indicator is provided merely as a model. The sample key indicators are not a checklist to tick off, nor do they indicate *everything* a Florida teacher should know and be able to do. Scrutiny of the *FEAP*s and sample indicators reveals important gaps.

It is ironic that in states like Florida, and elsewhere where high accountability for student learning is expected, the goal of student learning is not yet visible in the standards. Although systems of school grading, allocation of resources, student promotion, teacher rewards, and key education policies hinge on student test scores, the standards for helping teachers succeed in such a system have not yet adjusted.

At the time of this writing, a close examination of Florida's *Preprofessional Competencies* and the corresponding sample key indicators reveals little or no mention of student learning or the role of the teacher in student learning outcomes directly, although the word *learning* does appear in 40 instances (Figure 2.6).

Overwhelmingly, the emphasis, in the language of the *FEAP* standards, is on teaching and the role of the teacher. Teachers instruct, promote, and create. In AP #11, titled "The Role of the Teacher," *learning* is completely absent. Although the word is used twice in the actual names of two competencies (#7, "Human Development and *Learning,*" and #9, "*Learning* Environments"), learning in terms of *student learning* has been absent.

Linguistic analysis of the competencies and key indicators of *FEAP* identifies three uses of the word *learning*. In those standards, at the time this research was conducted, *learning* as

#	Competency	Learning as a verb	Learning as a noun	Learning as an adjective
1	Assessment			1
2	Communication		3	1
3	Continuous Improvement	1		5
4	Critical Thinking		2	1
5	Diversity			5
6	Ethics		2	
7	Human Development and Learning		1	3
8	Knowledge of Subject Matter		1	2
9	Learning Environments			7
10	Planning			4
11	Role of the Teacher			
12	Technology		1	
	Total	**1**	**10**	**29**

Figure 2.6 Analysis of *learning* in *FEAP*s.

a verb appeared just once. In AP #3, *learning,* in the form of action, is to be achieved by the candidate. "The preprofessional *learns* from peers and colleagues," according to this standard—an important concept and one that should surely be highlighted for preprofessionals in the initial stages of professional development. Missing from action, however, is an indicator that K–12 students, as the result of interactions with teacher candidates, also *learn.*

As an adjective, *learning* appears in the 12 standards 29 times, almost three times more often as a description of some other variable than as an outcome. Teacher candidates set up effective "*learning* environments" (AP #9) and design "*learning* activities" (AP #9). Clearly, the teaching process is associated with learning, but learning is not described as an end in itself.

To be fair, the *FEAPs* utilize synonyms to suggest student learning, terms such as *student performance, student progress, outcomes,* and *growth,* and every key indicator *implies* that the aim of teaching is to impact students as learners in a positive way. Four of the competencies—assessment, communication, diversity, and planning—come closest to naming what has become the ultimate measure of teacher effectiveness. Nine times the word *learning* appears as a noun: for example, "interactions are focused upon *learning*" (AP #2) and the candidate "communicates . . . high expectations for *learning*" (AP #2); but in the final analysis, a careful reader will agree that student learning as linked to teaching is a mere whisper, a ghost, a hint in Florida's standards. This is not to criticize the Florida ESC. In 1996, when 11 of these standards were adopted, teacher accountability for student learning was still a quiet expectation.

The point of my analysis is twofold. First, no set of standards is perfect. Standards are a slice from a larger entity, and they cannot possibly cover everything. Look closely, and you will realize what is not written but perhaps ought to be. Also, standards are not written in stone on the mountaintop; they continue to evolve, and as they do, they mirror society's demand for schooling. So, inevitably, standards change (see Researching Your Stance).

Happily, since 1996, one of Florida's *FEAPs* has been revised, and changes are apparent. In the fall of 2003, technology (AP #12) was modified and now includes the sole reference to "student learning" as a product ("The teacher identifies technology productivity tools to assist with the management of *student learning*").

RESEARCHING YOUR STANCE

1. Review your thinking about the qualities of good teachers and what you said in Chapter 1 about effective teaching. Quickly list the standards you believe might describe what a teacher should know and be able to do.

2. Find a copy of the *FEAPs*, located on the Florida Department of Education Web site (*http://www.firn.edu/doe/dpe/publications.htm*). Choose the appropriate standards for your level: preprofessional, professional, or accomplished.

3. Investigate the *FEAPs*. What standards or indictors do you especially applaud? What additional competencies would you want to see included?

Although the ability to foster high levels of learning for all students is yet to be clarified in all 12 *AP*s, Florida's *Sunshine State Standards* define what Florida's students need to learn and so serve to guide teacher and school planning.

Florida Sunshine State Standards

The **Sunshine State Standards** are Florida's version of statewide learning standards for students and are disseminated to all schools, defining expectations for student learning. Like the *FEAP*s, these standards were approved by the State Board of Education in 1996; they identify what Florida students should know and be able to do at certain stages throughout preK–12 grade levels.

In terms of organization, the language arts, mathematics, science, and social studies standards are clustered by grade level. Prekindergarten through Grade 2 is one cluster. Grades 3 through 5, 6 through 8, and 9 through 12 are other clusters. In addition, standards exist for the arts (dance, music, theater, and visual arts), foreign languages, health, and physical education.

The language of the *Sunshine State Standards* is not unlike that of other states, and an intricate numbering system was created to identify each of the original standards. For example, LA.A.1.3 identifies a reading language arts standard. The "subject" is identified first as an abbreviation. In this case, LA represents language arts. MA, SC, SS, DA, MU, TH, VA, FL, HE, and PE (mathematics, science, social studies, dance, music, theater, visual arts, foreign languages, health education, and physical education, respectively) are the subject areas represented. The *strand* comes next. It is an alphabetic label that represents a general category of knowledge within the subject area. In LA.A.1.3, the second *A* indicates that this is a *reading* standard. The term *standard* is a description of general expectations regarding knowledge and skill development within a strand. In LA.A.1.3, 1 represents the first reading standard: "The student uses the reading process effectively." Finally, the most specific level of information is the *benchmark,* a statement of expectations about student knowledge and skill at the end of one of four developmental levels: Grades PreK–2, 3–5, 6–8, and 9–12. In LA.A.1.3, 3 refers to the sixth- through eighth-grade cluster.

Originally, the clustering format was chosen to provide flexibility as schools and districts designed curricula appropriate for the needs of their students. As explained on the Department of Education Web site, it is expected that several benchmarks may often be combined into a single teaching or assessment activity. The listing of separate benchmarks does not mean that students must demonstrate achievement of them one at a time.

Contrary to some beliefs, although standards serve to distinguish essential knowledge and skills tested as part of a state's accountability system, *how* a curriculum is designed remains a local decision. Teachers who plan standards-based lessons make decisions, not about what to teach but about how to teach it. In the art of effective teaching, the best teachers design elegantly sequenced and richly relevant lessons.

According to Florida's Chancellor of K–12 Education, the *Sunshine State Standards* are now being reviewed and updated. Professional agencies, such as the Council for Basic Education, the College Board, the International Center for Leadership in Education, and other stakeholders have provided input and made recommendations about specific changes deemed necessary.

The intent of the revision process, according to the "Blueprint of Specifications to Guide Revisions," published in *Revising the Sunshine State Standards,* an electronic presentation by the Florida Department of Education (2005), is to reduce the number of benchmarks, create clearer spiraling across grade levels, clarify some of the language, and add more rigor.

The original standards were designed for curriculum developers, not teachers, and so they were never placed in an instructional context. General verbs were used to define learning, such as *understand* and *know.* The revised *Sunshine State Standards* will delineate rigor and relevance with closer attention to specific verbs: students will *analyze, evaluate,* and will demonstrate higher levels of knowledge and understanding. The new standards also aspire to define a more coherent progression of learning development.

The new benchmarks will be designed for direct use by teachers and will combine expectations for each grade level, reducing the number of currently existing benchmarks and focusing on vital core knowledge and skills. With a focus on inquiry and research, revisions will emphasize math and reading and limit other areas. The plan is that the new benchmarks and standards should take a teacher about 100 days to cover, allowing the remainder of the school year for review and for teaching material not delineated in the standards.

First-round revisions are being made to language arts and math. Science revisions will occur the following year. No plans exist at this time for adding prekindergarten, but eventually that will also occur. Final revisions should be in place by the time this book goes to press. Since the current *Sunshine State Standards* are now changing, be aware that aspects of the standards, such as details of the coding or identification system, are also subject to change.

Further information explaining the *Sunshine State Standards,* training for correlating instruction, and linking resources for classroom teachers can easily be located online. Some of these resources are listed and discussed in Chapter 6 of this book (also see Researching Your Stance).

RESEARCHING YOUR STANCE

1. Find a copy of the *Sunshine State Standards,* located on the Florida Department of Education Web site (*http://www.firn.edu/doe/curric/prek12/frame2.htm*) appropriate for your chosen level and discipline.

2. What are the strands?

3. What are the standards?

4. Choose a few benchmarks and analyze what they ask students at this level to know and be able to do.

5. Do not be afraid to take a critical stance. Again, what standards or indicators do you especially applaud? What additional competencies would you want to see included?

SUMMARY »»

After reading this chapter, you now know more about standards and how they guide learning. If you review your assumptions made at the start of this chapter (Taking a Stance), you may notice certain shifts. Now, in a final written reflection, you should be able to provide evidence that you have mastered the objectives of this chapter.

Take time to do the following:

1. Describe the connection between teaching and learning.
2. List and identify the key features of the *FEAPs*.
3. Explain your plan for passing the FTCE. What areas of knowledge are your strengths? In what areas do you need more experience? (See Researching Your Stance for assistance.)
4. List and identify the key features of the *Sunshine State Standards* as they relate to your teaching area.
5. As you compile a professional portfolio and draft various essays that demonstrate your pedagogical knowledge, describe your ideas at this point in your professional development for preparing students to pass the FCAT. How will you utilize your knowledge of standards as a guide? What aspects of the standards will you be sure to target?

℞ESEARCHING YOUR STANCE

1. Refer to a copy of the *FEAPs*, located on the Florida Department of Education Web site (*http://www.firn.edu/doe/dpe/publications.htm*). Choose the appropriate standards for your level: preprofessional, professional, or accomplished.

2. Analyze the *FEAP* standards and sample key indicators. Consider how you rate. To what degree are you knowledgeable, say, about technology (AP #12)? How much do you value students from diverse cultures (AP #5)? Can you plan interdisciplinary lessons (AP #10)?

3. Take time, at this point in your professional development, to assess yourself. Make notes describing what you know, can do, and believe right now. Focus first on your strengths. (AP #3 sets a standard for professional educators to monitor their own continuous improvement, building on current skills to set both long- and short-term goals.)

PREAMBLE TO CONTINUED READING »»

Why does a teacher's philosophy of education matter? For one thing, how teachers define learning and how they interpret standards determine what happens in classrooms. Consider these two deliberately extreme perspectives:

1. Standards are viewed as written lists of skills, representing a certain grade level and taught mostly from a publisher's textbook and other prepackaged supplemental

OUACHITA TECHNICAL COLLEGE

material. Students are drilled heavily and often are unmotivated. Teachers find that they have no time to "cover it all." In such a climate, standards are all-encompassing; teaching and learning is a linear path that ends with the dreaded FCAT.

2. Standards are viewed as basic building blocks and are taught in layers, integrated as developmentally appropriate into broader units focused on underlying concepts and values relevant to the learners. Students participate actively in constructing and monitoring their own progress, and teachers find that they are able to teach more critical and creative problem solving. In such a climate, standards are front-loaded, becoming part of an essential spiral, integral to a larger curriculum that includes various forms of assessment.

The suggested activities in Extending Your Stance will deepen your knowledge of standards. Pursue further the role of standards today and acquaint yourself with the national as well as state standards currently guiding teaching and learning in your field of education.

As you read Chapter 3, you will continue to consider where you stand on issues of teaching and learning. Hopefully, this book will help you view standards not as the ceiling, too high for some to reach, but as the floor, a foundation for building engaging, relevant, and substantial learning experiences that result in increased growth for all students.

EXTENDING YOUR STANCE

Standards written by various educational partners change with time.

1. Locate the specific subject area standards established by a professional organization akin to your discipline, such as the NCTE, NCTM, NCTSS, NAEYC, AAHPERD, IRA, and so on. Refer to Chapter 6 if necessary.
2. What is the date of their last revision?
3. Compare and contrast the national standards with the *Sunshine State Standards*.
4. Investigate other states and other standards, either for teachers or for students. What is the date of their last revision?
5. Compare the standards for your level and discipline. What do you see that is similar? What do you find different?

Chapter 3

Planning for Student Learning

Goals and Objectives

After reading this chapter, readers will be able to:

I. Know more about teaching and learning in a standards-based system.

    3.1.1 Explain the process of planning.

    3.1.2 Differentiate between goals, objectives, standards, and other components of effective planning.

II. Monitor personal, professional development.

    3.2.1 Write learning goals aligned with standards.

    3.2.2 Reflect on their methods for planning.

III. Refine personal philosophies for teaching and learning.

    3.3.1 Understand the importance of backward planning.

    3.3.2 Appreciate the role of assessment to guide good instruction.

This chapter is an introduction to the planning process. Rather than offer one template for how to plan, the discussion focuses on thinking about learning outcomes and methods for targeting growth in student achievement.

Taking a Stance contains a series of statements with no right or wrong answers. Take a few minutes to jot down your thoughts in response to these statements, and include some reasons for your beliefs.

Planning is a key part of teaching and learning, and educators plan using various tools. Philosophically, teachers hold different values as well. Compare your stance with those of others. Be sure to offer reasons for your feelings. As you read this chapter, try to adjust your current thinking to some of the expressed views of the profession at this point in time.

To what extent do you agree or disagree with the following statements?

1. Writing formal lesson plans is akin to busy work; most teachers simply do not have time to do it.

2. The best teachers are artists, born with intuition and a talent for creative planning, and the best teaching is often spontaneous, the result of an inspired response to immediate situations.

3. A good assessment plan is designed to give feedback to students.

4. It is critical that teachers treat all students equally.

The Importance of Planning

Think of important endeavors in your life, moments marked on a calendar, events that you may have dreaded or eagerly anticipated. Perhaps it was a major exam, like the GRE; or a big date, like your senior prom; or perhaps an exciting vacation, like a first trip to Europe. As you paid the registration fee and studied for the exam, purchased just the right outfit and decided with whom you would go to the dance, or bought the roundtrip ticket and outlined your itinerary for Paris, you did so willingly. Making large investments and spending precious hours planning are done readily to obtain desired results when things matter. The planning process for teaching and learning is no different, and teachers who have set high expectations for student learning plan carefully because they are intent on achieving results.

However, unlike soldiers marching toward battle against a state-mandated test, effective teachers are not robots. Teachers do not plan the same way. According to one veteran high school teacher, "It takes me a few hours at home on a Saturday to plan for the week. I teach three different preps, so I have to plan for three different classes." For myself, at the university level, and after decades as a teacher, I work in my office on campus, spending as many as 10 hours planning for one 3-hour graduate class.

Teachers do not plan the same way, but in their efforts to define, encourage, and assess student achievement, all effective teachers do plan carefully, and general principles apply (Erb, 2002; Gunter, Estes, & Schwab, 1999). The planning cycle involves a certain habit of mind and involves a series of professional decisions.

As part of the planning process, teachers make choices regarding setting standards for learning, aligning assessments, choosing a delivery model, rethinking procedures, and making accommodations. The process is recursive in that good teachers begin planning well before they ever enter the classroom. They continue to plan, monitoring and adjusting as needed, during the lesson; and they revise their plans, reconsidering strategies and making modifications for the next lesson at the end of the current lesson.

Knowing How to Begin

A Chinese proverb states that even the longest journey begins with a single step. Applied to the planning process, an inexperienced teacher might think that the first step involves finding an enjoyable activity, something sure to get students involved. However, while active learning is desired and fun is relished, learning may be lost. Another teacher may believe that the first step is located on page one of the state-approved textbook. Nevertheless, while text books are provided to frame curriculum, *learning is not packaged as part of the purchased materials.*

In other words, merely placing one foot in front of the other does not necessarily shorten the journey or get you where you want to go. Rather than wander aimlessly through a school year, textbook guide, or Internet site of cute teaching ideas, be a teacher who plans smartly, with purpose, conviction, and direction. Know how to plan for student learning. Reconsider the beginning by starting with the end.

Ironically, from the "certain habit of mind" perspective, the best-laid plans begin at the end (Wiggins & McTighe, 1998). The first step in planning with the end in mind is to know where you want to go. For example, returning to the GRE, prom, and Paris scenarios described earlier in this chapter, outcomes or aims might be identified, such as to score at least 1,000, enjoy that once-in-a-lifetime high school memory, or see Van Gogh's sunflowers in person. In teaching in a standards-based system focused on student learning, teachers begin planning by keeping in mind the learning outcomes they expect for their students.

The process is complicated and involves many factors, not the least of which is understanding the unique needs of the students to be taught and tailoring the instructional plan specifically for them. As such, the planning process takes considerable thought, and though not a linear, follow-these-steps kind of skill, it does begin with some understanding of the established standards, as well as other factors, including the context for teaching, the time constraints, the resources available, and so on.

Setting Standards for Learning

Considering the students they will teach, teachers set **goals** and **objectives,** linked to the *standards,* for what they want the students to learn. From the beginning of the planning process, teachers who plan with the end in mind identify their destination and the best way to get there. They name exactly what they want their students to know, believe, and be able to do as the result of the intended learning experience.

Goals.   Educational goals are umbrella terms, broadly structured, and take time to reach. A teacher may have very few goals targeted over several weeks, months, or year. Whether the goal is that students will develop a love of literature, become self-directed learners, solve problems using multiple perspectives, or understand scientific principles, the enormity of the goal means that it will take extended time and repeated teaching to achieve.

Objectives.   Educational objectives are narrower and more focused than goals, usually taught in a single lesson or series of lessons conducted in a relatively brief period of time. Objectives represent sequenced performances and identify the specific learning required to attain the goals. The ability to write clear learning objectives takes time and practice. Teachers have to think backward with the end in mind. They must analyze their goals, breaking down the larger learning and identifying discrete bits of knowledge and skill.

As suggested in an earlier example, a teacher may have to decide what is needed for students to develop a love of literature. In considering part of the many objectives helpful in reaching this goal, the teacher might write: "Students will identify six elements of suspense; they will diagram the plot of a short story; they will analyze the features of Edgar Allen Poe's 'The Tell-Tale Heart'; they will write their own suspense story; they will read their original story by candlelight to a group of peers using expressive pacing and diction; and they will appreciate the use of an unreliable narrator." Taken alone, an objective does not achieve the goal, but in combination, objectives begin to move closer to it.

Standards. The *Sunshine State Standards,* as well as local and national standards, help teachers select goals and objectives. Such standards have already been established and are an excellent place to begin making decisions about what will be taught. Standards should be consulted throughout the planning process to ensure that the educational goals and objectives set by the teacher are on track.

Although generic standards represent a beginning point in the planning process, they are not detailed enough to serve as the goals and objectives for learning. Teachers whose students achieve high learning gains understand that the established standards do not include everything, nor do they necessarily represent what their students need to know. Standards are not the final destination. They are more of a starting point, an outcome of the journey but, considered equally foundational, a place to begin building instruction customized for particular students. Effective teachers link their own goals and objectives, carefully designed according to the needs of their class, to the standards.

In planning this handbook, for example, I decided to deliberately target *FEAP #3,* Continuous Improvement, which states: "The preprofessional teacher realizes that she/he is in the initial stages of a lifelong learning process and that self-reflection is one of the key components of that process. While her/his concentration is, of necessity, inward and personal, the role of colleagues and school-based improvement activities increases as time passes. The teacher's continued professional improvement is characterized by self-reflection, working with immediate colleagues and teammates, and meeting the goals of a personal professional development plan."

Aligned to that standard, I wrote three goals for readers of this book: (a) to know more about teaching and learning in a standards-based system; (b) to monitor personal, professional development; and (c) to refine personal philosophies for teaching and learning. As I began to consider how to help readers attain these goals, I set specific objectives for each chapter. For example, the section you just finished reading was designed to help you develop "the ability to differentiate between goals, objectives, standards and other components of effective planning" (see objective 3.1.2 in the Goals and Objectives at the beginning of this chapter).

Learning to write goals and objectives to guide learning outcomes takes considerable practice, and Informing Your Stance contains an exercise designed to help you improve this important planning skill. Consulting local, state, and national standards is an essential part of the process. Standards will help you establish learning outcomes.

Aligning Assessments

Assessment is a vital part of the planning process and may even be the most important tool used by effective teachers. It is important to understand that *assessment* in this discussion is not the same thing as large-scale, high-stakes standardized testing, such as the FCAT. The distinction is important.

According to middle school veteran Julie Langston, "FCAT is one of those things we have to deal with. It happens every year, and I continue to teach regardless of its outcome. I look at scores to see if my students made gains, but I also look at a long list of other indicators to see if my students made gains. I realize that FCAT is just *one* of many ways to determine growth and learning. As with all tests or assignments, FCAT may not be the best test for any one individual, but it satisfies a group."[*]

Mandatory accountability tests like the FCAT support educational policy by summarizing data on large numbers of students. Such tests do not diagnose specific skills, monitor student processes, provide feedback about instruction, or inform teachers or individual students in ways that support teaching and learning. Those purposes are achieved by other measures, especially quality classroom assessments.

Classroom assessments, according to Richard Stiggins (1997), "provide the energy that fuels the teaching and learning engine" (p. vi). The primary purpose of good classroom assessment is to inform every decision a teacher makes. Unlike *grading*, or evaluation—which is always the province of the teacher, comes at the end of teaching, and provides evaluative feedback to students—assessment is an ongoing part of teaching and learning (Spandel & Stiggins, 1990), aligned closely with a teacher's aims and methods.

Assessment, like grading, may be considered the province of the teacher, but when done well, assessment, unlike grading, is also the role of the students. When assessment is shared

[*]By permission from Julie Langston.

between students and teachers, teachers come to see learning from the students' perspective, and this information provides invaluable knowledge about targeting and teaching for learning. When students assume some responsibility for assessment, conducting self- or peer assessments, for example, they understand better the features of achievement; they are able to monitor and adjust their own work; and they become more self-directed and independent. Unlike grading, an extrinsic motivator usually consisting of a system of rewards and punishments, student-governed assessment is intrinsically motivating, an essential instructional tool.

Assessment, like grading, may come at the end of teaching, but assessment is also continuous, occurring at the beginning and in the middle of lessons as well. As an integral part of teaching, assessment guides the planning process. From beginning to end, assessment helps teachers make decisions about the learning destination.

Before teaching, teachers, much like doctors who determine the nature of an illness before prescribing treatment, use **diagnostic assessment** methods. Assessments, such as pretests, surveys, interviews, observation, and any prior examination of student work, can diagnose or determine the prior knowledge and skill of students. Depending on what students already know, teachers can then adjust their plans or make modifications for individual needs.

High school teacher Tameka King reports, "I never plan a major unit I have met my students. I plan my lessons around the needs of my students—both emotionally and academically. I plan for the entire nine weeks at a time. I like to know what I want to cover, but I never know how I am going to cover it until I know the background knowledge of my new students. Every day I am learning something about my students, so how I may have taught something in years past may not be effective with my current students."[†]

During the lesson, formative assessments—designed to keep forming or shaping the learning—are used to monitor the process of student learning (Brancarosa & Snow, 2004). Even when done informally, formative assessments signal teachers regarding the pace and flow of a lesson, and the best teachers adapt their plans while they teach, clarifying, adding examples, helping individuals, and moving ahead accordingly, possibly pausing to reteach content as they go. Like diagnostic assessment, formative assessment takes many shapes.

At the end of the lesson or teaching unit, summative assessments summarize or evaluate what has been accomplished. Summative assessments are usually created for each objective and thus provide insight into the degree to which the lesson succeeded in helping all students gain the desired knowledge, skill, and belief.

According to first-year middle school language arts teacher Kristin Mudd, "I am constantly assessing my students informally. They receive daily grades based on their cooperation, involvement in the class, and evidence that they grasped the concept or objectives of the day's lesson. When it comes to formal assessments, it is all relative to the information being taught. During this first quarter alone, I have had the students write a formal expository paper, given an essay test on *Amistad,* and had the students give presentations on randomly selected nonfiction short stories."[‡]

[†]By permission from Tameka King.
[‡]By permission from Kristin Mudd.

In order to help you monitor your learning, several assessments are integrated into this book. For example, the purpose of Taking a Stance at the start of each chapter is to diagnose or tap your thinking before you are invited to read further and learn more. As checkpoints throughout each chapter, the Informing Your Stance, Articulating Your Stance, and Researching Your Stance boxes are designed to form and support your ongoing learning process.

In terms of summative assessment, if you are reading this book as part of a course requirement, your instructor may administer a test to determine how well you mastered its content. Each chapter ends with a "Summary" section containing questions designed to demonstrate your understanding of the chapter's objectives.

In a more practical or performance application, the portfolio pieces you may be writing to reveal your thinking as you read each chapter, or the final draft of your philosophy of education, will demonstrate your understanding after you have finished this book.

In terms of larger accountability, your ability to demonstrate the targeted *FEAPs* will also be made visible when you pass the FTCE or successfully complete your first year as a teacher. Ultimately, of course, the final assessment will always be your teaching effectiveness, residing in student results, not words. It is my hope that after you read this book, your students will be better able to demonstrate their learning, the results of your careful planning and inspired teaching, thereby showing the results of *your* learning.

Although assessments can be "graded," assessment is much more broadly construed. Like grading, assessment may give feedback to students, but it also provides feedback to teachers and is essential to good planning and instruction. Because ongoing assessment informs teacher decision making and is always focused on student learning, teachers know how to adjust their planning based on assessment data.

Teachers must match assessments to the goals and objectives of each lesson in order to monitor student progress. **Alignment** matching is like a constant compass check that keeps the learning moving in the right direction. Teachers must be able to use a wide range of assessment methods; they must also be able to choose the best method for assessing each objective.

Designing assessments that align with the learning goals and objectives is a complex task (Stiggins, 2001) requiring knowledge of numerous assessment strategies. For example, if the target to be assessed involves content knowledge, a simple multiple-choice, true-false, matching, or fill-in-the-blanks instrument may work. But if the target involves student attitudes, beliefs, values, or dispositions, an open-ended questionnaire or class discussion may be more helpful. Assessing the procedural domain, or student skill, usually requires observing behavior, performance, or a product.

Keep in mind that assessment has a profound effect on learning (French, 2003; Popham, 1999). For example, if students believe that factual knowledge will be assessed, then they may limit themselves to memorizing facts. Higher-order thinking and skilled performances that require application, synthesis, and problem solving should be an overarching goal for all instruction. Consequently, effective teachers strive to implement a range of assessment methods, paying extra attention to performance assessments (see Informing Your Stance).

Planning Procedures

As described above, teachers determine what will be taught based on prior assessment of student needs as linked to the existing standards, so that in a standards-based system of teaching, the framework for planning is established by aligning standards and assessment. But identifying standards will not ensure student learning, nor does assessment correlate to learning gains. Setting standards and aligning methods for demonstrating learning are essential parts of the planning process, but as James Britton said, "What the teacher does not achieve in the classroom cannot be achieved by anybody else" (Goswami & Stillman, 1987, p. iii.).

In the end, all learning is directly tied to the actual work of teachers. Teachers who know how to set goals for learning and then use assessment throughout the teaching process to diagnose, monitor, and ensure results understand that the heart of the work lies in implementation of the lessons, lessons aligned to the standards and the assessments.

So, the next step in planning is to determine *how* the goals and objectives will actually be taught. To establish a method of instruction based on assessment of students needs, teachers match the mode of delivery, including all teaching strategies, with the content. Planning the details of a lesson can be a time-consuming process, especially for the neophyte planner, but keeping the desired end in mind, coupled with careful decision making and detailed forethought, is likely to lead to the desired outcome.

Choosing a Delivery Model

Choosing the best learning model requires advanced knowledge of teaching methods. As Henry David Thoreau (1995) once said, "If the only tool you have is a hammer, then you tend to see every problem as a nail." Pity the students who have suffered from monotonous pounding! Artful teachers are able to select the best instructional tools, depending on the nature of the teaching challenge, for the job. The more methods, materials, resources, and techniques teachers can utilize, the more ably they can match instructional practice with aims, outcomes, and student needs. Versatility in the classroom results in motivated, engaged, successful learners.

Table 3.1 Instructional Delivery: A Sample of 10 Models

Cooperative Learning	Inquiry	Discussion	Concept Attainment	Direct Instruction
Problem-Based Learning	Lecture	Integrative Learning	Choral Response	Memory Recall

Delivery models (Table 3.1) change the nature of the teacher's and students' roles. Methods of instruction run the gamut from transmitting information (lecture) to independent inquiry, role playing, or collaborative problem solving. Choosing the most appropriate delivery model depends on many variables, including the time frame for the lesson, level of application targeted, and learning styles of the students, to name a few. Models of instructional delivery go by many names (Eggen & Kauchak, 2006; Gunther et al., 1999), but the point is that good teachers select a variety of instructional methods, depending on their aims.

Research on effective teaching methods appropriate for all grade levels and all subjects suggests certain best practices (Zemelman, Daniels, & Hyde, 1998). For example, Daniels and Bizar (1998) recommend that all teachers use integrative units, small-group activities, classroom workshops, authentic experiences, representing-to-learn, and reflective assessment. Basic principles of student choice, responsibility, expression, and community are implicit across their suggestions.

Learning about methods of instruction takes time. Beginning teachers tend to have smaller toolbags than veterans, and that is to be expected. As you think more deeply about the teaching and learning processes, try to notice not lesson plans that work but *strategies*. Do not be afraid to try new approaches. With the courage and creativity such efforts require, you will also need to be patient. Often, teachers must spend time breaking the nature of the learning experience into parts so that students understand and can do what is expected. For example, if you want to have a class discussion, and the students in your class have not had prior experience or lack the communication skills to participate effectively, you will need to spend several lessons teaching turn-taking, respectful listening, and so on (see Articulating Your Stance).

ARTICULATING YOUR STANCE

1. Continue to think about the goal you identified in Informing Your Stance (p. 35) and then assessed in Informing Your Stance (p. 38). How might you plan to teach this goal? What methods, strategies, and materials would you want to try?

2. Why do you feel that the methods you chose are the most appropriate for this goal?

3. Discuss your ideas with a partner. Together, brainstorm further instructional plans to help each other develop models of instruction likely to achieve desired student learning.

Rethinking Procedures

Because all planning decisions focus on student learning, the process allows ongoing revision, especially as the plans are implemented in the classroom. Carefully aligning assessments to the lesson targets and then using the data gathered, effective teachers are quick to adjust their plans. This flexibility is part of the art of good teaching, and the challenge is to switch gears, try a new angle, or respond to the surprises that arise without losing the focus of the lesson—the targeted learning (Wiggins & McTighe, 1998).

The opportunity to revise teaching procedures occurs in at least three points in the planning process and involves continuous assessment, as well as respect for the unexpected.

Point One.   Depending on diagnostic assessment, teachers revise their plans immediately before teaching. Often, assessments conducted the day before the lesson provide new insights and information concerning student needs, so teachers may adjust the intended outcomes of the lesson (perhaps raising or lowering the standard for achievement), their predictions about the amount of time needed to learn (either speeding up or slowing down the pace of instruction), and the method of instruction they believe most likely to result in high levels of student learning (more application or individual practice may be required).

Point Two.   **Informal assessment** is essential to effective teaching because it is the primary method for monitoring student learning. Such assessment should occur continuously during the actual teaching of a lesson. A few methods teachers may use to track the impact of the lesson include asking students questions; probing student thinking; watching body language and attitudes; and moving around the room, paying close attention to student participation. Effective teachers *use* the information gathered to make adjustments *while* teaching.

Point Three.   At the end of a lesson, assessment provides feedback to help teachers rethink their procedures. As one of my professors once said pointedly early in my teaching career, "Find out if your methods work. If they do, embrace 'em, but if they don't, chuck 'em out and try something else immediately!" Changes in plans do not necessarily need to be drastic. Revision is not about throwing away, but about adjusting and developing stronger methods.

The key to good teaching is to maintain an informed sensibility. As a reflective practitioner, you will want to analyze the assessment results at the end of a lesson. Ask yourself, "What went well?" Be able to cite evidence that what went well is directly linked to the aims of the lesson and student accomplishment. When surprises happen (and they will) and learning does not proceed the way you had intended (and it will not), immediately begin to plan for changes in the next teaching sequence.

Implementing assessment strategies takes careful thought. Sixth-grade teacher Julie Langston uses "student portfolios, projects, tests, essays, writing samples, and observations to assess learning." She explains, "Learning is a sloppy process. Students need room to make a mess and then clean it up and organize it in their brains. It's like renovating a room in your house. You gather all of your supplies and paint over the old color. Then you drag the furniture back in and move it around a while before you find where it fits. The students do the same thing with information. They have to compare it to the old 'stuff' they know and then find out where it fits."[§]

[§]By permission from Julie Langston.

Formal assessment methods such as **rubrics**, a name for a wide range of scoring guides, can be designed by the teacher to capture the messiness of student learning as a process as well as a final product. As a simple checklist for observations, a rubric might be something a teacher uses quietly, monitoring how well students participate during a group project, for example. Evaluating more structured evaluation in a uniform manner that links specified outcomes to, say, the completed project, a rubric can also offer concrete feedback to students.

Making Accommodations

Learners differ. They differ in their preferences and their academic strengths. They differ in their response to various instructional models. Some students learn best by working closely with others; some prefer to work alone. Consider different learning styles: visual, auditory, kinesthetic. Consider different intelligences: linguistic, logical-mathematical, spatial, bodily kinesthetic, musical, interpersonal, intrapersonal, existential, and naturalistic (Gardner, 1999). Learners also differ in their developmental growth. In any classroom, learners will differ widely in spite of their common ages, and many students will struggle with disabling factors that hinder their ability to learn in various contexts.

Students will have special needs, some less visible than others. An inclusive classroom means that all students, no matter what their disability, deserve to have the least restrictive environment and teaching that has been modified accordingly. In Florida, the percentage of students classified as disabled, according to the Individuals with Disabilities Education Act (IDEA), has been growing rapidly. More than 380,000 students with disabilities are taught in regular classrooms in the Sunshine State (Postal, 2004). All teachers, it follows, will have students with special needs mainstreamed in their classrooms.

Effective teachers understand the importance of varying instructional methods to meet the needs of all students. They also understand how to make accommodations, depending on the particular lesson, for individual needs in that specific instance. Based on their ongoing assessment, teachers adapt the content and method of every lesson to fit the needs of individual students. The teacher who lacks the necessary resources to help a particular student seeks help from others (see Researching Your Stance). The importance of collaboration is addressed in Chapter 6.

RESEARCHING YOUR STANCE

All learners have unique needs, depending on the nature of the situation. Choose one of the topics below to investigate further. See if you can learn more about the nature of students' learning needs and resources for making accommodations. Possible topics include but are not limited to:

1. Styles of learning. You might investigate visual, auditory, and/or kinesthetic learners.
2. Multiple intelligences. Research linguistic, logical-mathematical, spatial, bodily kinesthetic, musical, interpersonal, intrapersonal, existential, and/or naturalist intelligences.
3. Developmental growth. Research resources for developmentally appropriate teaching.
4. Disabling factors. See what you can find out about the IDEA.

Contextualized Learning

Early on, as part of the planning process, effective teachers become knowledgeable about the contextual features of the classroom, school, and community in which they teach. They become well acquainted with the culture in which they work, and they spend time getting to know the formal and informal policies girding their school site. As part of their learning, they analyze the demographic characteristics of the school, read the school improvement plan, and become familiar with the people in the larger school community. They identify the resources available and the support structure located in the community, including parents and other volunteers. They understand school policies for conflict resolution, student classroom behavior, individual education plans, and other special needs.

Learning does not happen in a vacuum. Scientific education research cannot be conducted in laboratories where all variables are controlled. In the complex world of teaching and learning, results are not generalizable. What works in New York City's urban schools may not be successful in the mountains of Colorado; methods that garner high results with preschool children will not necessarily transfer to adolescents; and practices designed to support certain disabilities are probably not the ones needed for the self-directed, gifted learner.

Students are the uncontrolled variable in any classroom. Not only do students in any given classroom differ from each other in terms of their interests, abilities, culture, needs, and personalities, but on any given day they also differ from the selves they demonstrated the day before. In other words, just because students were motivated or well behaved one day is no guarantee that they will be the next. Intellectual, physical, and emotional needs are subject to change, and good teachers are ever vigilant, carefully rethinking their assumptions (see Articulating Your Stance).

Prior knowledge plays a role in defining the ever-changing classroom context, and teachers constantly reassess in order to keep pace with shifting student needs. For example, in a biology lesson about marine animals, Jeremy—the slowest reader in the class—may surprise his teacher by knowing more about this particular subject than anyone else. Effective teachers understand that every teaching moment is likely to produce unexpected challenges.

Teachers dedicated to ensuring that all students achieve are sensitive to individual needs, and because they understand that learners are not the same, they do not treat all students the same way. Instead, teachers committed to the notion of equity are careful to ensure that all

---

ARTICULATING YOUR STANCE

Consider the role of classroom management in effective planning and instruction.

1. What are the potential hot spots in the plans as you have been developing Articulating Your Stance (p. 39)?
2. What special needs might your students have in order to participate successfully in this lesson?
3. What can you do, while planning or teaching, to ensure that classroom management goes smoothly and all students are able to participate fully?
4. Discuss your ideas with a colleague.

students have the same opportunities to learn, and they work hard to advocate for special resources and additional support for any student who may be underserved, have a unique need, or require extra help of any kind. Using different resources and differentiating methods as necessary for various student needs, effective teachers help all students learn.

Literacy is the Language of Learning

The standards and accountability movements, as well as the increased importance of literacy in a technological society (Myers, 1996; Selber, 2004), have raised the demand for higher levels of literacy in all citizens. For example, the abilities required to read on the Internet differ from those needed for conventional text (Corio, 2003). Increasingly, students must demonstrate sophistication as readers and writers or they are not permitted to graduate from high school. Literacy is no longer the responsibility of English language arts teachers.

Helping all students read, write, speak, listen, and think critically has become everyone's job (Delbridge, 2002), and school partnerships increasingly make literacy their primary goal for improvement. Teachers at all levels and in all disciplines are regarded as teachers of reading and writing.

Parents, too, want to know how to help their children be more successful in school. Because "learning in school focuses on the mastery of academic language as the primary language of thought" (Myers, 1996, p. 291), an increased emphasis must be placed on language skills in multiple situations. The more opportunities children have to speak, listen, read, and write for a variety of purposes and audiences, inside as well as outside of school, the more likely they are to be successful learners (Zemelman et al., 1998).

Because literacy is a tool for learning, and because students need to be able to use the tools of language in different contexts, all teachers should consider themselves to be teachers of language (Brancarosa & Snow, 2004). Literacy is an important thread to weave into every teaching and learning experience. Such integration means that teachers consciously target specific language behaviors at the same time that they address other learning objectives, and they tell students at the start of every lesson what they will be learning about listening, speaking, reading, writing, or thinking. In classrooms where teachers and students view literacy not as a school subject, the sole domain of the English language arts class, but as an important part of thinking and learning, teachers can expect increasingly sophisticated language performances from their students over the school year.

ESOL: Meeting the Needs of Florida Students

Effective schools set high standards and expectations for all students, no matter where they come from, and demonstrate respect for diversity, especially for different cultures and languages (Suárez-Orozco & Suárez-Orozco, 2001). Correspondingly, effective teachers welcome students with all abilities and all languages, and then work to design classroom experiences that foster second-language acquisition and learning.

In Florida, one of five states in the country with the highest percentage of English language learners (ELLs), chances are good that you will teach either in a multilingual classroom or have students, either non-native English speakers or with limited proficiency in Standard English, who have special language needs (Beers, 2004). All teachers in Florida are expected to be able to work successfully with ELL students, and Florida's Performance Standards for Teachers of English for Speakers of Other Languages (ESOL) provide a blueprint.

The ESOL Competencies for Florida's Teachers of English, for example, specify that teachers need to create a positive classroom environment that accommodates the learning styles and cultural backgrounds of students. They must be skilled at reducing cross-cultural barriers between students, parents, and others in the school, and they must be able to use formal and informal methods of assessing the needs of ELL students and then plan and teach accordingly.

Addressing the ESOL standards requires strategic teaching and special attention to your own patterns of communication (Peterson & Salas, 2004). Such instruction is not intended to lower the standards of what is taught but rather to provide a scaffold for helping students as they learn in an unfamiliar language. Five basic premises (Herrell, 2000) for supporting and enhancing instruction for ELL students, whenever possible, in *any* class are the following:

1. Use language the students can understand. To provide comprehensible teaching, the teacher must use vocabulary and concepts that the student can decode.
2. Provide many opportunities for students to talk. Increased verbal interaction is integral to classrooms where teachers encourage all students to participate in discussion, conversation, and other oral activities.
3. Provide background information to make language learning less demanding. Contextualizing language makes it easier for students to understand new words and new concepts.
4. Use grouping techniques and other forms of social support to reduce students' anxiety.
5. Use active learning and encourage the participation of all students, especially ELL students.

According to Danling Fu (2004), teaching English language students via lecture, whole-class instruction, or sessions comprised of just one activity is less successful than designing interactive small-group lessons using multiple methods. Effective teachers individualize their instruction and are willing to make special accommodations in order to help ELL students learn.

The International Teachers of English to Speakers of Other Languages (TESOL) organization has developed standards and assessments for teaching PreK–12 ELL Students. Further information can be located at their Web site: *http://www.tesol.org*.

The Role of Technology

Learning in the 21st century is very different than it was historically (Myers, 1996), due in part to the advent of new technologies in the digital age (Selber, 2004). For example, with the new communication capabilities, learning is no longer limited to a fixed location but can happen anywhere at any time. Multimedia education is also resulting in innovative instructional designs and is changing the shape of traditional classroom experiences (Daniels & Bizar, 1998).

The turn-it-on, plug-it-in, or use-it-wireless revolution has evolved to the point where schools are now equipped with, and teachers and students have access to, technological applications (Wallace, 2004). Possibilities for enhancing teaching and learning abound, limited only by teachers' imaginations. For instance, technological tools such as cameras, audio and video recorders, CD-ROMs, interactive white boards, laptops, e-books, and other computerized technologies are available to support students as they create sophisticated representations of their knowledge.

Current research in new media demonstrates that innovative learning opportunities are changing the nature of teaching and learning. In one particular application, student blogging, using online personal journals, Web logs, or blogs, has many benefits, including increased student interest, participation, ownership, diversity of opinions, and subject matter knowledge (Ferdig & Trammell, 2004).

Technological applications exist for every possible need. Teacher professional development, for example, can be customized via online training and management, as evidenced in the ETS "System 5" program. Specialized software and interactive Web sites provide information, resources, and services with the click of a mouse.

Technology has changed the way teachers and parents communicate as well. Classroom telephones, cell phones, e-mail, personal digital assistants (PDAs), and Web sites have become common vehicles for increased family involvement in the day-to-day life of schools and classrooms. Technology applications provide abundant information—a marvelous support for beginning teachers seeking materials, methods, or background facts.

Technology is also a critical resource for assisting students with special needs. Assistive technology exists for students with dyslexia, hearing problems, cerebral palsy, Parkinson's disease, speech disorders, or any other disability. Online classrooms, as well as the use of voice recorders, adapted pencil grips, writing keyboards, and voice output devices, are some of the technological tools that can be utilized (Cavanaugh, 2002). Teachers who advocate for higher learning for all students do not hesitate to find and secure technological assistance for students in need (see Articulating Your Stance).

ARTICULATING YOUR STANCE

Once again, consider one of the goals you selected in Informing Your Stance (p. 35). Figures to target, assess, teach, and modify in your imagined classroom scenario. Talk with a colleague and discuss your ideas.

1. What instructional approaches would you choose to attain your goal?
2. What methods and materials seem especially appropriate? Why?
3. What special accommodations might be required, depending on the needs of your students?
4. What strategies would you use to help a student whose first language is not English?
5. Finally, how will technology enhance the implementation of your lesson?

SUMMARY »

After reading this chapter, readers should be able to demonstrate increased knowledge of the planning process and the components of effective plans. The following prompts may help you show your mastery of the chapter's objectives.

1. Imagine that you have been asked to speak to a group of novice teachers about the planning and teaching processes. You will have only 10 minutes to discuss the key elements of effective planning.
2. Design a graphic or concept map reflecting your view of the planning process or create an analogy, an extended metaphor, to describe it in familiar terms.
3. What is the difference between goals, objectives, and standards?
4. What is the role of good assessment?

PREAMBLE TO CONTINUED READING »

Extending Your Stance contains suggested activities to help you think more critically about the planning process.

Good teaching is the result of good planning, and learning how to plan well is an art that takes time to develop.

- Begin with knowledge of standards and spend time thinking about multiple ways to use assessment as windows on the learning process.
- Acquaint yourself with various methods and materials, and do not hesitate to learn all you can from more experienced teachers. Pay close attention to your students. They will help you see what methods work best for them.

EXTENDING YOUR STANCE

1. If possible, observe a classroom teacher who is teaching an actual lesson. What informal and formal assessments did the teacher use?
2. What other features of planning are evident in the instruction?
3. Afterward, interview the teacher. Ask, "What went well?" Listen to the teacher's reflections, noting especially what sources of evidence are cited. Are they linked to the aims of the lesson?
4. Ask, "What surprised you during the lesson?"
5. Ask, "If you could do it again, what changes would you make?"
6. Revisit your initial assumptions made at the start of this chapter (Taking a Stance). Reflect on any shifts in your assumptions.

- Sometimes planning can feel like an arduous chore, an assignment perhaps to satisfy a professor in a college course or a school administrator. Those new to the teaching profession may feel confused by what they perceive to be mixed messages about form or content, and it can be frustrating to work with experienced classroom mentors who seem never to write a word or do any visible planning at all!

- Good planning is an individual process that can take many shapes, depending on the teacher's needs and the writing situation. A lesson plan left for a substitute, for instance, must be more detailed than one you write for yourself. Plans written to demonstrate your effectiveness to others—administrators or faculty, for example—may have to conform to a particular style.

- Above all, good planning is a way of thinking. Teachers who focus on helping all students achieve high learning gains share certain habits of mind. As they plan, they set clear learning goals and lesson objectives. They design developmentally appropriate learning experiences that utilize the best practices. Because they do not treat every learner the same way, they make modifications for individual needs. Throughout the process, they draw on many formal and informal assessments to monitor the results, using their new knowledge to refine and improve their planning decisions. The cycle is intriguing, illuminating, and inspiring. Effective teachers are rarely bored, and consequently, neither are their students!

As you read Chapter 4, you will have the opportunity to take a closer look at some sample lesson plans. See what components of standards-based teaching and learning you recognize.

Teaching for Student Learning

Goals and Objectives

After reading this chapter, readers will be able to:

I. Know more about teaching and learning in a standards-based system.
- 4.1.1 Identify elements of standards-based lesson planning.
- 4.1.2 Analyze features of lesson plan formats.

II. Monitor personal, professional development.
- 4.2.1 Design detailed procedures for lessons.
- 4.2.2 Design developmentally appropriate and interdisciplinary lessons.

III. Refine personal philosophies for teaching and learning.
- 4.3.1 Relish the role of teachers as curriculum planners.
- 4.3.2 Synthesize components of effective teaching.

This chapter is an exploration of classroom applications. Five interdisciplinary lesson plans are presented as examples of standards-based curricula that address Florida's *Sunshine State Standards*.

No discussion of teaching and learning is complete without concrete, relevant examples. So, now that we have reviewed accountability, assessment, standards, and elements of the planning process, it is time to take a closer look at some actual lesson plans.

First, consider your perspective on the statements in Taking a Stance.

To what extent do you agree or disagree with the following statements?

1. Teachers should be hired because of their expertise in a content area. It is not their job to teach other subjects.

2. Effective teachers teach to the standards established for the subject and grade level at which they are hired to teach.

3. The problem with active learning is that it takes too much time. Besides, teachers do not have the luxury of using creative activities. They are required to prepare students for the FCAT.

Five Sample Lesson Plans

As you gain experience in curriculum planning, you will find that certain habits of mind become second nature. Over time, you will begin to discover that you have internalized detailed procedures, methods for delivering instruction, and strategies for making adjustments. Your classroom will begin to run "like a well-oiled machine" (Wong & Wong, 2004) as you find that you are able to organize, plan, and think without needing to write everything down.

But early in your career, planning is a form of professional writing. Effective teachers know that planning with the end in mind takes time. It is a sophisticated mental process that does not happen just because you care about your students. It comes with the discovery of writing, with close observation of multiple assessments, with reflection, and with experience. Do not let the planning process discourage you! It is only a matter of practice until you will begin to see the results of your efforts.

By way of application, and to help you think more practically about the art of planning, this chapter includes five lesson plans that address Florida's *Sunshine State Standards*.

Even though all of the plans describe in detail the procedures for teaching and assessing specific aspects of learning, you will notice that each plan looks different. For example, one plan uses a split-procedures box, detailing what the teacher will do in one column and what the students will do in the other; another plan blocks sections of the lesson. In other words, the format for lesson planning is not standardized. Effective teachers develop their own model for writing a lesson plan or are flexible about using the template that may be required by a principal or administrator.

Each lesson targets a specific grade level, from early childhood, elementary, middle, and high school. All plans are framed by standards-based teaching, beginning with identifiable objectives or standards that name what students will learn and ending with a form of summative assessment. Each lesson is also set within the framework of research-based instruction.

The five lesson plans provide examples of curriculum design, representing a teacher's habit of mind that supports student learning. Each plan demonstrates one of the following components of standards-based thinking: goals and objectives focused on specific content knowledge, literacy skills integrated into the content, different models of instruction, a range of performance assessments, and various accommodations for student needs.

Content Area Teaching

Each lesson plan is designed specifically to teach the *Sunshine State Standards* in one content area: social studies, language arts, math, health, or science. Goals and objectives are aligned with these standards (and linked to other national standards).

Interdisciplinary Applications

In addition to content knowledge, each lesson integrates literacy, targeting a language skill: speaking, listening, writing, critical thinking, or reading comprehension.

Delivery Model.   The instruction in each lesson uses different delivery models: problem solving, memory recall, concept attainment, collaborative groups, and discovery (Gunter et al., 1999).

Assessment.   Formal as well as informal assessments—each designed to match objectives—illustrate a range of possible ways to document student learning: analytic trait assessment, self-assessment, holistic portfolio assessment, peer assessment, and attitudinal assessment.

Accommodations.   Each plan also attends to the teaching context and the specific needs of representative students. Accommodations, modifications, and adaptations are suggested for special needs that include ELL students, those with behavior management problems, and gifted, visually impaired, or alliterate students.

Early Childhood and Elementary Examples

According to the National Association for the Education of Young Children (NAEYC), teachers plan instruction that is developmentally appropriate. Teachers who work with elementary and preschool children are especially knowledgeable about the needs of young learners. As early as kindergarten, children arrive at school with varying levels of knowledge and skill. Almost any elementary classroom contains students with varying levels of ability.

Experienced elementary teachers understand that learning is developmental, and rather than setting their standards on a particular grade level and then teaching all children to those universal standards, they differentiate instruction, modifying it for individual learners.

In its position statement defining effective curriculum, the NAEYC lists features like "valued content is learned through investigation and focused, intentional teaching" and lessons are "tied to the daily activities of children."

The two lesson plans in this section are aimed at children in the primary and elementary grades. "Speak Up! Sharing Responsibility and Classroom Duties" is designed to

---

|NFORMING YOUR STANCE

Take a close look at the next two lesson plans, designed for early childhood/elementary-age learners.

1. Which lesson plan format is easier to follow? Why?
2. If you were the substitute teacher in these two classes, would you be able to implement these plans? Why or why not?
3. If you were a principal evaluating these two teachers, based on the evidence they present in these plans, what would you consider their strengths? What suggestions would you make for improvement?

---

introduce concepts of civic responsibility to first graders. "Listen and Learn: Memorizing the Parts of Speech" is designed to help third graders understand various functions of language.

Both lesson plans share basic elements of planning with the end in mind, and both integrate standards from different disciplines (see Informing Your Stance).

Sample Lesson Plan: **Early childhood example**

Speak up! Sharing responsibility and classroom duties

A first-grade social studies lesson

Context for teaching the lesson: This lesson is intended to be taught during the first few days of the school year, ideally close to Labor Day. Children are probably still getting acclimated to first grade and to each other. Perhaps they are still learning how to speak and listen appropriately in a large group. Depending on the logistics of time and student needs, this lesson will most likely need to be taught over several days.

Rationale: This lesson, part of a larger Civics unit, uses a problem-solving approach to help young children identify safety and cleanliness issues in a messy classroom and understand everyone's role in keeping their classroom safe and clean. The lesson integrates social studies, problem solving, and speaking skills and results in a group plan for assuming shared responsibility for maintaining a clean, well-organized classroom.

First-grade students, especially ELL students, may be reluctant to participate orally in class discussions, or they may be overly eager to speak and not yet gracious about taking turns. At the start of the school year, procedures are being learned and students may still be relatively inexperienced at understanding the culture of a school.

Sunshine State Standards: The following goals and objectives are linked to Florida's *Sunshine State Standards* for early childhood. Corresponding benchmarks from social studies, language arts, and health education are cited in parentheses.

Students will:

Goal 1. Demonstrate methods for getting along with others.

> **1.1** Take turns in conversation (LA.C.3.1.3).
>
> **1.2** Work with one or more people toward a common goal (HE.C.2.1.5).
>
> **1.3** Use a problem-solving approach (LA.C.1.1.1).
>
> **1.4** Stand to speak (LA.C.3.1.1).
>
> **1.5** Speak so that others can hear (LA.C.3.1.1).
>
> **1.6** Demonstrate features of a good speech, including eye contact and gestures (LA.C.3.1.4).

Goal 2. Demonstrate responsible citizenship.

> **2.1** Recognize the commemorative holiday known as Labor Day (SS.A.5.1.3).
>
> **2.2** Define *community* (SS.C.2.1.3).
>
> **2.3** Define *responsibility* (SS.C.2.1.1).
>
> **2.4** Name the responsibilities of school employees (SS.C.1.1.5).
>
> **2.5** Identify their individual rights and responsibilities (SS.C.2.1.1).
>
> **2.6** Clean the classroom.

Goal 3. Appreciate shared responsibilities.

> **3.1** Compare responsibilities between home and school (SS.C.1.1.3).
>
> **3.2** Understand the responsibilities of school authority figures (SS.C.1.1.5).
>
> **3.3** Appreciate how different workers benefit the community (SS.C.2.1.3).
>
> **3.4** Work with others to clean the classroom.
>
> **3.5** Share their appreciation for the school custodian.

Curricular Connections: Talk together about the different jobs, roles, and responsibilities that various people in their families and in the community have.

Also, depending on the day this lesson is taught, be sure that students understand the concept and history of Labor Day as a commemorative holiday.

Always falling on the first Monday in September, Labor Day, a national legal holiday, honors workers in our society. More than 100 years after the first Labor Day observance, there is still some doubt as to who first proposed the holiday for workers.

The first Labor Day holiday was celebrated on Tuesday, September 5, 1882, in New York City, with a parade to honor the working class. This was sponsored either by the Knights of Labor or the Central Labor Union. In 1884 the first Monday in September was selected as the holiday, as originally proposed, and labor unions urged similar organizations in other cities to follow the example of New York and celebrate a "workingmen's holiday" on that date. The idea spread with the growth of labor organizations, and in 1885 Labor Day was celebrated in many industrial centers of the country.

Today, Labor Day is observed not only in the United States but also in Canada and other industrialized nations. While it is a general holiday in the United States, its roots in the working class remain clearer in European countries.

It has come to be recognized in the United States not only as a celebration of the working class, but even more so as the unofficial end of the summer season. In the northern half of the United States at least, the summer vacation season begins with Memorial Day and ends with Labor Day.

Getting Ready to Teach: Wait to assign classroom jobs to the students. Allow the room to remain messy for a period of time—perhaps for 1 day or until you cannot stand it any longer! Be sure to collaborate with the custodian, agreeing to let the room remain untouched overnight in preparation for the custodian to attend class as a guest speaker.

Materials: Visual cards for how to be a good speaker and listener, chart paper, markers, crayons, index cards, and a book for reading aloud. *Swimmy* by Leo Lionni (1968) or *Together* by George Ella Lyon (1989) are both good choices.

IDENTIFYING THE PROBLEM

1. Explain to the children that you are getting ready to have a class discussion. Review classroom rules for respectful speaking and listening.

2. As the children get settled at their desks and become quiet, get their attention and say very seriously, "We have a big problem in our classroom community." Wait and then say, "I wonder if you know what it is."

3. Have them think, pair, and then share their ideas with a partner.

4. After everyone has talked to someone, ask them to sit quietly again. Allow the problems to arise from the students. Remind them that everyone who wants to talk will have a chance and that they will need to raise their hands and be patient, awaiting their turn.

5. After a range of problems has been identified, if the targeted problem (the messy classroom) is not noticeable enough, suggest that students look around at the classroom. Ask them to describe what they see. As students take turns sharing what they notice, be sure to ask them to stand when they speak.

6. Nod and point as, one by one, the students mention paper on the floor, books out of place, desks out of order, and all the other messy features you have allowed to accumulate. Nod and agree, saying, "Yes. You have found the problem in our classroom community." "Yes. That is a good observation. The trash can does need to be emptied." "Yes. Good thinking. The books on the floor are a safety problem." Receive and validate every contribution by repeating it, agreeing, or praising.

7. Nudge those who haven't spoken by asking, "What else do you notice? Let's take turns sharing."

CONSIDERING POSSIBLE SOLUTIONS

8. After all the noticeable problems have been identified, say, "You are all right! This classroom is a terrible mess, and I do not know what to do about it. *We* have a problem in our classroom community, and I need *your* help to solve it."

9. Ask the students to think quietly and then make suggestions about what could be done. One by one, invite them to come to the front of the class and offer their ideas while you write each contribution exactly as it's given on a large chart tablet. As you write the children's words, be sure to repeat them loudly, reinforcing word recognition.

10. Once a list has been collected, say, "Let's think about it some more [take a recess or lunch break], and I'll invite [NAME], our school custodian, to talk with us about your solutions."

11. When the class returns from the break, have the school custodian come in as a guest speaker. Hold up picture cards that demonstrate how to be a good member of an audience: sitting still, eyes on the speaker, hands resting on laps.

12. Introduce the custodian and have the children introduce themselves to the custodian too. Review the features of a good speaker, using picture cards: eye contact, clarity.

13. Show the custodian the list of solutions. As you review the list, point to each word and speak clearly.

14. Ask the custodian to describe the job of cleaning the school. Encourage children to ask questions until all have a good understanding of the custodial responsibilities.

15. Be sure that the children understand that too much needs to be done every day for one person to handle it all. Keeping a clean school is everyone's responsibility.

16. Thank the custodian for coming. Ask each child to say "thank you" for [name one thing the custodian does for our school community]. Use visual cue cards to support the speaking if needed.

17. Review the possible solutions and *agree as a class to take turns helping*. With partners, students should clean up the mess.

18. This is another possible break. Students can be thinking about jobs that need doing every day and every week.

MAKING PLANS FOR SOLVING THE PROBLEM

19. Brainstorm a list of responsibilities students have at home for helping to keep their homes orderly and clean (making the bed, feeding the dog, picking up belongings). Write those on the board.
20. Now brainstorm class roles, that is, jobs that need doing, and write the jobs on different colored index cards (large ones).
21. As you hold up the cards, say the words and ask the class to repeat each one.
22. Hand out the cards, one per child, and ask them to draw a picture of what the word/job involves. Possible jobs include paper monitor, table washer, pencil collector, librarian, and so on.
23. As they finish their pictures, tell the students that everyone will take turns sharing. This time, they get to be the guest presenter. Remind them that good speakers stand without fidgeting, look their audience in the eye, and speak clearly so that everyone can hear.
24. Ask each student to stand at the front of the room and describe the responsibilities of the named task. Or you can place a sturdy box, at or a small podium, at the front of the room and invite them to give a speech explaining the duties of a class citizen. (Some people say that they stand on a "soap box." Not really, but speakers do stand at podiums or other raised platforms.) Use cue cards if needed.

IMPLEMENTING THE PLAN

25. Agree as a class to begin immediately.
26. Post a chart delineating jobs and listing students (plan to rotate jobs each day or week so that everyone has a turn to do everything). Stop here and clean the room if needed.

EXTENDING THE LEARNING

27. Talk to the students about the progress they are making in terms of being responsible for keeping the classroom community clean.
28. Review the concepts of community and responsibility. Continue to help the students understand what a classroom community should look and sound like, and also what individual and shared responsibilities in a classroom mean.
29. As a culminating activity, and as another way to review and assess understandings, read aloud a children's book that illustrates the concept of sharing responsibilities or working together to get things done. Students can look for examples of community, responsibility, similarity, and difference.

George Ella Lyon's *Together* is a good choice because the two girls share responsibilities for getting things done. The girls are similar in that they both help out, but they are different too. One is African American and one is white.

Leo Lionni's *Swimmy* is another good example because the little fish learn to swim together in defense against the big fish. Swimmy is also similar to the other fish but has a different color.

ASSESSMENT

Much of the assessment in this lesson will be done informally. You will need to monitor participation closely, noticing which students seem to understand and providing extra help to those who don't.

As you pay attention to their performance, gently remind students when necessary to think of a solution, to take turns listening and speaking, and to stand or speak up when it's their turn.

As a follow-up to the content knowledge presented in this unit, continue to review with the class, asking certain students to define the Labor Day holiday, to name the custodian, to define *community,* to explain what the word *responsibility* means, and so on.

Over time, you will also be able to track the degree to which individuals assume responsibility in the community.

Be sure to give a lot of positive reinforcement, especially as students speak willingly or help to clean the room.

Formally, one performance should be assessed with a closer look at the traits demonstrated.

Using an analytic trait scoring guide (Figure 4.1), make a written note on each student's speaking abilities. Three scores (posture, eye contact, clarity) should be documented per child. These scores can serve as a diagnostic indicator of individual needs. Continue to build increasingly sophisticated speech acts and create multiple opportunities for students to participate in a community where everyone has a voice.

TRAIT	3	2	1
Posture	Stood willingly, no prompting needed, and did not slouch or fidget	Somewhat reluctant to stand and speak; may have rocked back and forth or been otherwise distracted	Hesitant, perhaps unwilling to stand and speak or display extreme nervousness
Eye Contact	Looked directly at the audience	Looked at the audience some of the time	Did not make eye contact with the audience
Clarity	Audible to everyone	Spoke softly or inaudibly in part	Inaudible

Figure 4.1   Analytic trait rubric for speaking.

MODIFICATIONS FOR ELL STUDENTS WITH LIMITED PROFICIENCY

To reduce the anxiety of ELL students, do not require, force, or coerce them to speak at first. But in this lesson, by the time the custodian comes to the classroom, every child should be feeling comfortable enough to stand and say his or her name. Also, the focus on vocabulary specific to the classroom jobs provides a context for ELL students to understand. Pointing at the problems as students make initial contributions also supports the second language learner, and writing and repeating for everyone to see provides increased comprehensible input.

Sample Lesson Plan: **Elementary example**

Listen and learn: Memorizing the parts of speech

A third-grade language arts lesson

MATERIALS

Class copies of the poem "The Old-Fashioned Rules of Grammar"
Students will need paper and pencil.
Teacher will need to use the board.

OVERALL OBJECTIVE

This lesson integrates strategies for listening and memorizing with a quick grammar lesson that introduces the parts of speech.

Anticipatory set: Read aloud the poem "The Old-Fashioned Rules of Grammar." Then ask students to tell you what they remember from it. When they are finished naming all they remember, compliment them: "You remembered a lot about this poem!" Tell them that today they are going to learn some strategies for *really* remembering things!

STATEMENT OF OBJECTIVES AND PURPOSE

Students will use listening strategies effectively (LA.C.1.2); understand that words function as parts of speech, depending on how they are used (LA.D.1.2); and develop some confidence in their ability to remember information (mnemonic devices).

Instructional Objectives	Procedures	Expected Pupil Outcomes	Method of Evaluation
Students will listen attentively to the speaker, including making eye contact and facing the speaker (LA.C.1.2.4).	"Today we are going to memorize all the parts of speech and their definitions." Write *fly* on the board.	Students will listen attentively and understand that the function of a word depends on its usage.	Informal teacher monitoring: Remind students to look at you and listen attentively.
Students will understand that there are patterns and rules in the syntactic structure, symbols, sounds, and meanings conveyed through the English language (LA.D.1.2.1).	Ask, "Is this a noun or a verb?" Write three sentences: *The fly buzzed. Planes fly. He caught a fly ball.* Explain that words do different jobs, depending on how they are used. In the first sentence, *fly* works as a noun, naming an insect. In the second, it's a verb, showing action. In the third, it serves as an adjective, describing the kind of ball.	Students with behavior management problems could be invited to act out the sentences.	Ask students to name other words that function differently, depending on their use. Another way to think of it is to think of words, like *run*, that have multiple meanings. Check orally to see that students understand this concept.
Students will differentiate between *hearing* and *listening*.	Write *hearing* and *listening* on the board. Ask, "What part of speech are these words?" "Yes, it depends on how they are used." (Students can give examples). Everybody act out: *Students are hearing what the teacher says.* Now act out: *Students are listening to what the teacher says.* Discuss how these two words seem similar but are actually different skills.	Students will name effective listening strategies, such as making eye contact and facing the speaker (LA.C.1.2.4).	Teacher observation.

(*continued*)

Instructional Objectives	Procedures	Expected Pupil Outcomes	Method of Evaluation
Students will be able to name and cite examples of the parts of speech.	Now, *listen* this time. Listen very attentively as I read the poem again. This time, see how many parts of speech and examples you can remember.	Students will name and cite the parts of speech.	Self-assessment on a piece of paper.
Students will consider using a mnemonic device to memorize a portion of a poem.	Explain that they are now going to memorize the entire poem, with help from their classmates and from some mental techniques. Ask the students to name techniques they have used in the past to try to remember something: phone numbers, a poem, addresses, people's names, spelling words, a song, multiplication tables, lines for a play, whatever. Affirm their answers. "Yes, you listen closely, repeat it over and over, have a friend give it to you, look for patterns, make up a story, act it out, use rhythm and rhyme . . . "; include all possibilities. Pass out the copies of the poem (number the stanzas). Divide the class into partners or groups of three, depending on the class size. Assign one stanza per group. Tell them that their job is to memorize their stanza and to see what memory devices they can use.	Students will participate in the discussion. Those with behavior problems will be partnered with students more likely to stay on task. Finally, students will take turns, in small groups, reciting their stanza from memory and then reporting to the class what strategies they used.	Informal teacher monitoring and peer assessment.

Figure 4.2   Poem for a lesson plan.

THE OLD-FASHIONED RULES OF GRAMMAR

A noun is the name of anything, as *SCHOOL* or *GARDEN, HOOP* or *SWING.*

Adjectives describe the kind of noun, as *GREAT, SMALL, PRETTY, WHITE* or *BROWN.*

Instead of nouns, the pronouns fit, as *HE, YOU, THEY* or *IT.*

Verbs tell of something being done, to *READ, WRITE, JUMP* or *RUN.*

How, when, or where, the adverbs tell, as *SLOWLY, NEAR, NOW* or *WELL.*

A preposition stands before a noun, as *IN* or *THROUGH* a door.

Conjunctions join the words together, as *AND, BUT, SO* or *WHETHER.*

Interjections show surprise, as *OH*, how pretty! *AH*, how wise!

Three little words you often see are articles *A, AN, THE.*

The whole are called the parts of speech which reading, writing, speaking teach.

Author Unknown

Closure: In a choral reading, students will stand, without notes, and perform the entire poem (Figure 4.2) from memory. Students will be able to participate especially well on their group's stanza or part of speech. Finally, for self-assessment purposes, you might ask students to take out a piece of paper and number it from 1 to 10. Ask them to evaluate their ability to learn by listening, to explain what they have learned about memorization, and to see if they can now list the parts of speech and give one example of each.

Middle School Example

According to "This I Believe," a position statement of the National Middle School Association (NMSA), every adolescent "must be engaged in learning that is relevant, challenging, integrative, and exploratory." Sue Swaim, the executive director of the NMSA, writes about the issues inherent in teaching young adolescents. She quotes John Lounsbury, one of the founders of the middle school movement, who argues that teachers in middle schools have "inescapable responsibilities for developing well-educated adults who are also healthy, ethical, and productive citizens" (Swaim, 2005).

In the face of high-stakes testing and other accountability issues, middle school educators, like teachers at most levels, struggle to balance what they know and believe

Take a close look at the middle school lesson plan.

1. In what ways might features of this plan be considered "relevant, challenging, integrative, and exploratory"?
2. Compare this plan to the first two. Talk with colleagues about aspects of the plans that you applaud. Feel free to offer modifications and suggestions.

about good instruction with narrowly defined and easily measured standards. Planning lessons that meet these somewhat disparate aims is indeed a challenge. The lesson plan in this section, "What a Concept! Analyzing Mathematical Thinking," was designed for use in a sixth-grade classroom. It incorporates a student-managed portfolio assessment as a vehicle for demonstrating analytic thinking (see Articulating Your Stance).

Sample Lesson Plan: **Middle school example**

What a concept! Analyzing mathematical thinking

A sixth-grade math lesson

Before teaching this lesson: Institute a bell ringer assignment, to be done at the start of each day's lesson. Give students a daily problem to solve, and be sure to draw from a wide range of mathematical skills. These problems can serve as review, applied practice for a current skill, or introduction to new topics. You might incorporate student names, current events, other real-world situations, or mind-bending puzzles.

Stress that what matters in the working of the bell ringer is not just right/wrong answers but also the *mathematical thinking* behind the solutions. Encourage students to take risks, to try various approaches, to monitor their own thinking, and to feel comfortable about using writing to explain. Let them know too that eventually they will be required to turn in a portfolio, their collection of the daily bell ringers.

Purpose of this lesson: Using concept attainment (Gunther et al., 1999) as a model of instruction, this lesson provides students with an opportunity to synthesize their daily bell ringers, organize their portfolio prior to submitting it for a grade, and explicate their understanding of larger mathematical concepts.

PROCEDURES

What the teacher will do	What students will do
1. Begin with a *daily bell ringer.* Write a problem on the board: *Dinner at Charlie's Café costs $12.00. Sales tax is 7.5%. What was the total bill? And if you want to leave a 15% tip based on the total bill, how much money will you leave?*	1. Students will arrive at the class.
2. Ask students to copy the problem from the board.	2. Students will take out a piece of paper and begin to copy the problem.
3. Ask students to get to work solving the problem.	3. Students will work on the problem.
4. Walk around the room and watch as students solve the problem.	4. Students will ask for help if they are stuck.
5. Help students if necessary. Ask them to think about another possible way to solve it. "Consider possibilities" or "Don't be afraid to start over," you can say.	5. Students will try another method for solving the problem.
6. Remind them that this is at least a two-step problem. First, calculate the tax and then calculate the tip. Answers will start with a dollar sign.	6. Students will finish the problem.
7. Tell students to write down their thought processes.	7. On the second half of their paper, students will write a paragraph explaining their thinking, showing *how* they worked the problem.
8. Invite someone to give the answer for the tax problem and to tell the process used.	8. As a student explains his or her answer ($12.80) and how he or she solved the problem, others will check their work.
9. Have a second person share his or her process.	9. Students may use the overhead or board to show their work to the class, if needed.
10. Invite another student to report his or her work on the tip problem.	10. Another student shares ($1.92).
11. Ask another student to explain another way to solve the problem.	11. Different strategies are demonstrated.
12. Tell students the etymology of *tip*. From Old English, originally an acronym, "TIP" was written on a box and placed on a pub's bar for patrons to insert	12. Students listen and discuss.

(continued)

OUACHITA TECHNICAL COLLEGE

What the teacher will do	What students will do
money "To Insure Promptness." Discuss current connotations and the importance of rounding up.	
13. Ask students to take out their math portfolios and add today's paper to the back.	13. Students take out their portfolios and add their work.
14. *Introduce today's lesson:* an analysis of mathematical concepts. Ask students to take out a piece of paper.	14. Students take out a piece of paper.
15. Have students brainstorm as many words identified or associated with mathematics as possible.	15. Students list as many items associated with math as possible. They think of everything they know about math.
16. If they are having trouble with this, help them begin by analyzing the items/elements from today's bell ringer.	16. Students add to their list: tax, money, percent, multiplication, addition, estimates, and so on.
17. Continue nudging students until they have a *comprehensive* list. If necessary, have students share five items with a friend.	17. Students add to their lists.
18. Once students have listed as many terms as possible, ask, "Do any of these items seem to belong together?"	18. Students review their lists, noticing similarities among items.
19. Ask students to now group those things that are alike in some way.	19. Students group items that are alike.
20. Tell them to try to find several different groups.	20. Some students may draw circles; others may rewrite. Grouping strategies vary.
21. Ask students to label the groups by defining the reasons for grouping.	21. Students name their groups and write reasons.
22. Have some students share. Accept all answers, as long as students are applying generalizations and inferences to their groups.	22. As a prompt for those having trouble and as a check to see that everyone is articulating reasons for groups, a few share their methods.
23. Ask students to group or subsume individual items or whole groups under other groups. Ask, "Are there items in one group that you could put under another group?"	23. Students continue grouping and labeling.
24. Monitor student work by checking to see that they have been able to generate a wide variety of math items and then group the items.	24. Students compare their work.
25. Say, "Now that you have demonstrated remarkable skill at identifying common concepts, let's apply the same thing to your portfolios. Please get them out."	25. Students get out their portfolios.
26. Say, "Take the forty to fifty bell ringers you have solved and explained (or however many you have done), and group them according to a system of mathematical concepts. You will need to identify at	26. Students listen to directions.

least three groups and no more than six. Arrange these papers into the categories and put them back into the portfolio with dividers between the sections."

27. Show students colored paper you have hole-punched, ready for this purpose.

27. Students notice the colored paper.

28. Then show them how to write a cover letter addressed to you, explaining how they chose to arrange their work and why.

28. Students ask questions about the assignment.

29. Write directions on the board or post them on an overhead.

29. Students reread the directions.

30. Pass out a copy of the holistic rubric (Figure 4.3) and the midterm grading procedure.

30. Students look at the grading procedure.

31. Help students prepare their work for turning it in.

31. Students prepare their portfolios.

SUNSHINE STATE STANDARDS

MA.B.3.3.1 Students estimate measurements in real-world problem situations using money.

MA.A.5.3.1 Students understand, apply, and explain theories related to numbers using concepts about numbers.

LA.B.1.3.2 Students use writing processes effectively, using support that is substantial, specific, relevant, concrete, and/or illustrative.

LA.B.2.3.1 Students write to communicate ideas and information, demonstrating comprehension of experiences.

LAD.2.3.1 Students select language that shapes reactions, perceptions, and beliefs.

Extending the lesson: Introduce the students to a marvelous new book, perfect for them, and all about today's lesson. Lisa Papademetrious's *Sixth-Grade Glommers, Norks, and Me* (2005) is chock full of analytic thinking. Allie, the main character, is trying to understand the very different world of middle school. In this book, she makes a mental list of all the students she knows and then creates categories. The *glommers* are girls who cling to each other in groups; *norks* are a combination of nerd and dork; and, worst of all, *squashes* are crushes that make you feel as if you heart has been stepped on.

Adaptation for gifted students: Advanced students should be challenged to look especially closely at their groupings. They might, for example, use the *Sunshine State Standards* as a conceptual framework, applying their own work to six of the categories created by the state: number sense, concepts, operations, measurement, geometry, spatial sense, algebraic thinking, data analysis, and probability. Or they could use portions of the organizing structure of the course textbook as a framework for their portfolio. They could be invited to add charts, graphs, or other visual, artistic representations of their mathematical thinking.

Assessment: Grade the portfolios using a holistic scale (Figure 4.3).

Figure 4.3   Holistic rubric for portfolios.

6	5	4	3	2	1
Sophisticated	Accomplished	Proficient	Literal	Developing	Limited
An exemplary performance; original work; an orderly display of data; well written; mature conceptualization of problem solving and advanced mathematical understandings.	Portfolio demonstrates clear reasoning of significant mathematical concepts; work is well detailed and proof that this student has taken some genuine risks.	Daily work is complete; portfolio is organized in logical categories; all writing demonstrates mathematical thinking.	Daily work reflects some moments of genuine effort but is sometimes inaccurate. The portfolio is organized; attempts to apply theories but lacks details.	Portfolio reflects some effort to solve problems and explicate process, but insufficient evidence exits.	Missing or incomplete. Bell ringers; little or no organizing structure; letter to the reviewer is illegible or underdeveloped.

High School Examples

Educational reformer Ted Sizer has conducted research and written extensively about the quality of learning in American high schools. According to Sizer's Coalition of Essential Schools, high schools should be guided by a few relatively simple principles. Especially important to a standards-based model of teaching and learning is the idea that students should not be promoted because they get older, nor should they be retained because of one low test score. The ultimate demonstration of learning is exhibitions of their work. What matters is a visible outcome that demonstrates knowledge and skill (Dykema, 2002; Sizer, 1996).

John Goodlad, another noted reformer, also writes about methods for improving high schools. He has called for a complete redesign of instructional methods. Goodlad's ideas, like Sizer's, echo John Dewey in their insistence that learning is best accomplished when connected to real problems (Goodlad, 1984).

High school reform may very well be one of the most current and pressing issues in education, at least according to the 2005 National Governors Association summit, where Microsoft Chair Bill Gates called for an increased emphasis on the "Three R's: *rigorous* curriculum, made *relevant* by excellent teachers, in a setting in which personal *relationships* create a welcoming learning environment" (Landgraf, 2005). According to a report released by the ETS, a 5-point "Action Agenda" was also produced at the National Governors Association summit. Designed to guide systematic high school reform nationwide, the points included an emphasis on higher standardards, high-level knowledge, and increased accountability (Landgraf, 2005).

The two lesson plans in this section are modeled on theories of relevance. "School Violence: A Critical Conversation" is a 9th-grade lesson plan integrating critical thinking with issues of personal safety, and "Discovering Theories About the Nature of Energy" is an 11th-grade lesson featuring student-conducted inquiry to investigate principles of physics.

School violence: A critical conversation

A ninth-grade health lesson

Lesson Target	To take a critical look at issues of personal safety and school violence.
Sunshine State Standards	The student knows how to use effective interpersonal communication skills that enhance health (HE.B.3.4).
	The student understands the possible causes of conflict among youth in schools and communities and knows positive communication strategies for preventing conflict (HE.B.3.4.6).
	The student knows ways to effectively express feelings and opinions on health issues (HE.C.2.4.2).
	The student knows ways to work cooperatively with others to advocate for healthy individuals, schools, and families (HE.C.2.4.5).
	The student uses responsive listening skills, including paraphrasing, summarizing, and asking questions for elaboration and clarification (LA.C.1.3.4).
	The student asks questions and makes comments and observations that reflect understanding and application of content, processes, and experiences (LA.C.3.4.2).
Materials	Copies of Todd Strasser's *Give a Boy a Gun* Feedback checklist
Student Assessment	This collaborative lesson uses peer assessment to provide feedback formatively as part of the Socratic Circle process (Copeland, 2005). The rubric (Figure 4.4) is reviewed at the start of the lesson, used during the lesson, and discussed after the lesson in order to accurately reflect the nature of the activity as it developed.

(continued)

Prelesson	Prior to this lesson, students read Todd Strasser's (2000) young adult novel *Give a Boy a Gun*. Dedicated to ending youth violence, the novel presents the multiple perspectives of a fictionalized account of a high school shooting. As students read, they take notes, keeping a journal of their responses. Strasser's book is an excellent resource for secondary students, including a list of Web sites and print resources for further information. For visually impaired students, the book will be read either in Braille or by listening to a taped recording.
Lesson Goals	Although plenty of good literature tackles the theme of school violence, providing complex substance for class discussions, text alone will not provide the answer(s). As Strasser himself writes in the novel's closing, "Anyone looking for one simple black-and-white answer to the problem of school violence . . . will not find it here" (p. 143). Collaborative discussion serves as a window for thinking and talking in a meaningful way.
Body of Lesson	"Today we will be discussing *Give a Boy a Gun* in order to gain insight into the complex and critical issue of school violence in our society. "The discussion method we will be using is known as "Socratic Circles," named in honor of Socrates, the Greek teacher. What do you know about his method of learning? "Yes, Socrates lived in ancient Greece over two thousand years ago, and he believed that lecturing someone was not an effective way to teach. He believed in questioning, using student talk as a way to think more deeply and more critically about important issues. "Everyone will be participating in the discussion, not to debate or argue points, but to consider multiple perspectives on this difficult topic. As with any good discussion, we do not know in advance where it will lead us. We will begin by talking about the reading you've done and then take it from there." Pass out the rubric (Figure 4.4) and discuss the standards for a good performance. "With your permission, rather than explain the process too much beforehand, I'd like to just get started and explain the rules as we go. Okay? "Are there any questions? Good, then let's try it." Randomly divide the class into two groups. You can do this by asking students to think of the last digit of their phone number. Those with odd numbers stay in their chairs. Those with even numbers move to the inner circle. The inner circle will sit in a circle on the floor in the center of the room. The outer circle will sit in desks in a circle surrounding the inner circle. The students in the inner circle read an excerpt from the text aloud, and then they engage in a discussion of the text for approximately 10 minutes. They can use their books and their notes. If they need help beginning the discussion, be prepared to ask them an open-ended question. If their discussion stalls, be ready to ask a question from your seat outside of both circles, but resist the urge to participate. Your job is to keep the discussion on track, nudging the students to participate by asking questions to prompt their talk if needed.

While the inner circle discusses the book, the outer circle must sit silently. With rubrics in hand, they listen carefully and observe the performance of the inner circle. It may also be helpful if they make notes.

After 10 minutes, stop the discussion and ask the inner circle to sit quietly while students in the outer circle now talk for 10 minutes about how the discussion went. Their feedback is not on content but on the discussion process, and they can use the features of the rubric as a guide. One way to get this feedback to work is to take turns, asking each student to make an observation. Stop the feedback process after 10 minutes. Ask students to change places and roles. The new inner circle now holds a 10-minute discussion followed by 10-minute feedback provided by students in the new outer circle.

Postlesson

Discuss the process with students and decide as a class on the next steps regarding school violence. Perhaps you will survey others and map the school to find out how students and teachers perceive safety issues in your school (Wood, 2005).

Name_____ Date_____

Please make notes on the performance of the inner circle.

Characteristic	Superb	Adequate	Problematic
Participating equally			
Listening respectfully to others			
Speaking clearly			
Focusing on the subject			
Referring to the text			
Summarizing key ideas			
Asking questions			
Making comments			
Sharing personal connections			
Connecting to bigger issues			
Expressing feelings and opinions			

Overall, what went well?

What surprised you?

If they could do it again, what should they do differently?

Figure 4.4 Peer assessment for the Socratic Circle.

Sample Lesson Plan: **High school example**

Discovering theories about the nature of energy

An 11th-grade physics lesson

Description of the lesson: This lesson draws heavily on the Suchman inquiry model (Gunter et al., 1999) and is designed to engage students in reading and conducting an inquiry into any topic. For purposes of this example, a lesson suitable for an 11th-grade science class, the topic is related to the nature of energy.

Rather than assume that information is limited to textbooks or experimentation, this lesson integrates reading as an important strategy scientists employ to investigate scientific problems which seem to have no definitive solution. It is designed to be implemented across the arc of the unit.

SUNSHINE STATE STANDARDS ADDRESSED:

SC.B.1.4   The student recognizes that energy may be changed in form with varying efficiency.

SC.B.1.4.1   The student understands how knowledge of energy is fundamental to all the scientific disciplines (e.g., the energy required for biological processes in living organisms and the energy required for the building, erosion, and rebuilding of the earth).

SC.B.1.4.2   The student knows that the structure of the universe is the result of interactions involving fundamental particles (matter) and basic forces (energy), and that evidence suggests that the universe contains all of the matter and energy that ever existed.

SC.H.1.4.1   The student uses the scientific processes and habits of mind to solve problems.

SC.H.1.4.3   The student understands that no matter how well one theory fits observations, a new theory might fit them as well or better, or might fit a wider range of observations, because in science, the testing, revising, and occasional discarding of theories, new and old, never ends and leads to an increasingly clear understanding of how things work in the world, but not to absolute truth.

LA.A.2.4   The student constructs meaning from a wide range of texts.

LA.A.2.4.7 The student analyzes the validity and reliability of primary source information and uses the information appropriately.

1. **Setting up the lesson:** Prior to the start of a unit, as early as a week or two before the unit is scheduled to begin, administer the open-ended pretest (Figure 4.5) to students. Explain that because this is a *pretest*, they should write what they think and know *now*. Their thoughts at this point in time will serve as an entrance to the unit. They are safe not knowing something, but they should answer each question as best they can, since their answers will be used to plan another lesson.

2. **Class brainstorm:** After students have completed their individual responses to the above pretest, collect their papers and guide students as they brainstorm answers to the second question as a whole class. Once again, tell them, "Think about what you already know about the nature of energy and brainstorm things you hope to learn." Encourage students to formulate a long list of questions about the topic. Accept all contributions, and write each question on the board or overhead.

3. Collect and capture the class brainstorm, and use these data, coupled with the pretest data, to write a series of questions for students to research. The topics should take the form of problems that need further research, avoiding topics that can be easily answered or solved (*What is a calorie?*). In other words, allow the nature of the topics to be open-ended, genuine problems with multiple possibilities.

4. Write each question/topic in the form of a scenario. For example:

   Energy can be found throughout the universe. Recently, however, scientists have reported larger levels of energy in the Earth's upper atmosphere. What might account for this dramatic increase?

   Students will each require their own scenario, so you will need to devise a healthy list.

What do you know about <u>the nature of energy?</u>

What do you want to know about <u>energy?</u>

How do you propose to find out?

By the way, how do you feel about *reading* as a way to learn more about energy?

Figure 4.5   Pretest for a lesson.

5. Assign inquiry scenarios by matching particular problems to individual students. Pay attention to the expressed interests of students, using the pretests as a guide, but also think about individual skill and motivation. Although the time this requires is extensive, the careful selection and matching of problems with students is critical.

6. Launch the unit by explaining the inquiry process and presenting the students with their individual scenarios. Reassure them that their problems are not easily answered, and that the point is not to come up with one pat answer but to find out all they can that helps them to understand the problem.

7. **Time to conduct research:** Allow considerable class time for students to conduct the necessary research. Provide them with resources, including textbooks, journal articles, a classroom library, a school media center, and electronic databases. Their assignment is to familiarize themselves with the subject. Tell them to read and conduct necessary research in order to prepare a datasheet. The datasheet is intended to serve as a resource during the question-and-answer session that will follow.

8. Collect the datasheets, and work with students who seem reluctant or hesitant until everyone has finished. Check for gaps in datasheets and steer students toward other resources, if necessary. Extend the research time.

9. Finally, select a student with a detailed datasheet to be the first Class Leader.

10. **Present the process:** Explain the rules (Figure 4.6) to the students. The Class Leader will be the primary source of data but can only answer questions with "yes" or "no."

11. The Class Leader distributes the problem in written form to the class and then reads the problem statement aloud.

12. **Gather facts:** The students are required to phrase questions that become hypotheses. If the questions are not stated correctly, the Class Leader will ask students to rephrase them so that they can be answered either "yes" or "no."

    Your job, as teacher, is to help by reminding students that what they are asking is part of the answer, but it needs to be restated in light of what they already know.

The rules

Students may ask questions when called upon by the Class Leader.

Questions must be asked so that the answer is either "yes" or "no."

Students may continue to ask questions if they get a positive response.

Students may talk with each other only during caucus periods, the times for group discussion.

The teacher will provide follow-up information if deemed necessary.

Figure 4.6 Class rules for a lesson plan.

In other words, each question is worded as a tentative hypothesis, and the important part of this activity is for students to struggle with the process. As teacher, resist the urge to tell them *what* they are trying to say but help them decide *how* to say it.

When the questioning stalls or a particularly engaging moment occurs and students simply need time to discuss in more detail, either the Class Leader or the teacher calls for a caucus. Set a time limit, 2 minutes perhaps, and allow students to talk freely among themselves before continuing with questions.

13. Students record the data as they are uncovered. These notes can also be made by the teacher on the board.

14. **Develop a theory:** Questioning the Class Leader for data ends when a student suggests a theory. Write the theory on a separate section of the board.

    At this point, the class must decide if the theory should be accepted or rejected. To verify the theory, students continue to ask questions, but now the questions are designed to consider various conditions, for example, intended to prove or disprove the theory.

15. **Evaluate:** After the group verifies a theoretical answer, discuss the theory in more detail. Consider its rules, effects, and applications. Talk with the students about the nature of theory and the scientific process they just conducted. Together, decide on methods for improving the activity and encourage students to take more responsibility for the process.

16. Establish a plan for the other scenarios and assign Class Leaders, perhaps one a day for a portion of each class, for the duration of the unit.

17. **Assess the learning:** As a culmination of the unit, after the last scenario has been presented, administer the following posttest (Figure 4.7) to students. Remind them that the questions should look familiar, as this little test is parallel to, and in fact practically identical to, the pretest they took at the start of the unit. They should make every effort to demonstrate their learning as the result of the daily discovery lessons.

Closure: For comparative purposes, return pretests and ask students to share any shifts they may notice. Be sure to talk with the students about their new insights, attitudes, and beliefs about the nature of science, the role of reading, and their increasing ability to solve problems (see Informing Your Stance).

What have you learned about the nature of energy?

What have you learned about scientific theory?

By the way, how do you feel about *reading* as a way to learn more about science?

Figure 4.7   Posttest for a Lesson Plan.

SUMMARY ➤➤

After a close examination of the sample lesson plans in this chapter, you have a more concrete understanding of standards-based teaching and learning. If you review your initial assumptions made at the start of this chapter (Taking a Stance), you may notice shifts in some of your thinking. Take time to demonstrate your understanding of this chapter's objectives and your increasing skill as a curriculum planner.

Complete Extending your Stance and use it as an artifact in your professional portfolio to show your emerging skills in planning for student learning.

PREAMBLE TO CONTINUED READING ≫

In this age of high-stakes testing, more than ever, quality teaching is predicated not on some arbitrary statement of what should be taught at each grade level, but on what we know about how students learn. The best teachers take a developmental perspective, paying more attention to cognitive stage theories than to age or grade-level planning (Daniels & Bizar, 1998).

- Students differ, and so do the methods employed by effective teachers.
- The best way to produce high levels of learning in students at any grade level is to engage them in experiences that shift the responsibility for and the challenge of learning to the students themselves.
- Interdisciplinary, multimodal lessons include accommodations, not for all learners, but for the those of the population being taught.

In Chapter 5, you will have the opportunity to take a reflective stance—a second, more critical look at the plans presented in this chapter—a chance to push your thinking about effective planning and instruction a bit further.

Reflection

Goals and Objectives

After reading this chapter, readers will be able to:

I. Know more about teaching and learning in a standards-based system.
    5.1.1 Describe the role of reflection in the teaching and learning cycle.
    5.1.2 Explain methods of self-assessment for teachers as well as students.

II. Monitor personal, professional development.
    5.2.1 Plan methods for collecting and analyzing data.
    5.2.2 Draft a formal philosophy of education.

III. Refine personal philosophies for teaching and learning.
    5.3.1 Revise earlier beliefs about teaching and learning.
    5.3.2 Evaluate different models of lesson plans.

This chapter—which argues that the best use of assessment is to inform teaching and thus impact learning—is closely linked to the *FEAP*s that address assessment and continuous learning. The reflective process is defined as a way of seeing more clearly the connection between teaching and learning.

Before you consider the ideas presented in this chapter, consider the statements in the Taking a Stance box. Take a few minutes to jot down your thoughts. Be sure to offer reasons and examples to explain your feelings.

In a very real sense, part of an educator's job is to enable students to lead happy and productive lives. As a teacher educator working in the state of Florida, my aim is to enable my students to become teachers who have happy and productive careers, careers that reward them not with high salaries or public acclaim, unfortunately, but with the sense of having made a difference in their students' lives. Daunted by the challenges of the profession, I worry about the future of my students, and I wonder how I can help them be fully prepared for long, satisfying careers as professional educators.

As a future classroom teacher, you too want to be effective, the kind of teacher who truly makes a difference in lives, not numbers. What does that mean in a standards-based system? *Is it enough to understand the role of standards, to dedicate oneself to student learning, or to plan with the end in mind?* Many talented teachers quickly realize that their knowledge and skill in teaching and learning are *not* enough, and they leave the profession burned out or, perhaps saddest of all, they stay, counting the years until retirement, mere shells of their former selves.

Especially alarming in this day of acute teacher shortages, researchers report that it is the *youngest* teachers who have the highest attrition rate. In the departure decisions of young teachers who graduate, self-efficacy and doubt about their effectiveness play a significant role (Goddard, Hoy, & Hoy, 2004; Ingersoll, 2001).

According to a policy brief on internal accountability published by the Consortium for Policy Research in Education, when student achievement is a goal for a school, teachers have increased enthusiasm and feel satisfied by their results (Fuhrman, 1999). Goal-setting theory (Locke & Latham, 1990) supports the understanding that teachers who believe their work will result in demonstrated student learning achieve long-term professional satisfaction.

But how do teachers know when they have done their jobs well? Being able to see, with any clarity, the results of our work seems especially difficult. I have observed several beginning teachers in action who, when asked how it went after teaching a marginally successful lesson, have said, "Fine! It went really well! The students all said they loved it." Conversely, I have observed many veterans who were discouraged at the end of an otherwise successful lesson because one small detail did not go as planned. Both perspectives are understandable, given that teaching is by definition an act of optimism conducted by people who care deeply about excellence.

Balancing optimism and a false sense of accomplishment with disappointed perfectionism, or even wallowing in the perception of failure, might seem to merit professional counseling, but another option is available. Rather than sail though the teaching process in superficial bliss or drown in discouragement, effective teachers strive to be reflective about their practice.

What is reflection? In what ways does it support a teacher's sense of well-being? How does reflection support the connection between teaching and learning? What are some ways of developing a reflective habit of mind?

Reflecting on Teaching and Learning

Educators appear to agree that **reflection**, an important part of effective teaching, is a means for helping teachers know when practices are going well, but reflection means different things. Discussions about reflection are ongoing and pervasive in the professional literature, and few conclusions have been reached. I would not presume to provide a definitive response to the complexities of reflection, but I believe reflection is essential in the quest to improve student learning, and I offer a few thoughts about the process.

Defining the Reflective Process

Reflection is often defined, in general terms, by citing John Dewey and Donald Schön. According to Dewey (1963), education is a process of deriving meaning from personal experience, but experience alone does not constitute learning. To understand the significance of the experience to us personally, we must reflect. Thinking reflectively, in Dewey's words, means that we are "willing to endure suspense and to undergo the trouble of searching" (p. 16). The reflective process, a search for understanding, cannot happen without the experience. Reflecting on experience, as defined by Schön (1984), can occur in two ways: (a) reflecting-in-action and (b) reflecting-on-action.

For example, imagine that one morning when you wake up, get dressed, and leave your house, you step off the front porch and into a mud puddle. What a way to start your day! You must go back inside, change your socks or stockings and shoes, and start all over again. What an experience! Now pretend that the next morning you are especially tired when you wake up, and as you leave you house, you mistakenly step into the same puddle and must go through the same terrible process all over again. Dewey would point out that you have had some experiences but have not yet learned from them. Schön would add that you need to think more carefully either in retrospect, after you've had the first experience, or in introspect, as you are leaving the house but before you step off the porch.

Reflection as conscious, deliberative actions and reactions is a process of inquiry that guides teachers to constantly analyze and use information about the teaching and learning experiences. Reflective teachers thoughtfully plan before teaching (reflection-on-action), readily monitor and adjust their plans while teaching (reflection-in-action), and consider the results of their work after teaching (reflection-on-action).

Reflective thought, conceptually as well as practically, can be a somewhat vague aim. Just as experience alone does not constitute learning, neither does reflection alone. The reflective practitioner needs something to reflect about. Assessment provides data—documented experience, fodder for reflective thought, and the means for achieving the specific aim: understanding the teaching experience through the lens of student learning (see Informing Your Stance).

Assessment in a Reflective Model of Standards-Based Learning

For teachers in standards-based systems, assessment has become a primary responsibility (McMillan, 2001), and as educators grapple with ways to transform the teaching/learning process in order to meet the standards (Mentkowski, 2000), they discover that assessment

¶NFORMING YOUR STANCE

Often the deepest learning happens in retrospect. Think of a lesson learned in your life. When did it happen, what did you learn, and what caused the learning?

1. Describe the experience that led to the lesson. Try to pinpoint the moment when the learning or insight occurred.
2. What prompted your learning? What data or evidence helped you to see or think more clearly about the experience?

is also a primary tool for achieving quality in both product and process. The critical role of the teacher in assessing students is no longer implied or considered as an afterthought; more than ever, teachers need to be highly skilled uses of knowledge and tools to use assessment in a continuous, ongoing fashion.

Assessment has become a professional imperative. Incorporating methods of assessment into teaching, aligning assessments with standards, creating an assessment system to manage the data on individual students, and using the data to effectively inform teaching decisions are challenges that exist throughout the field (Falk & Ort, 1998; Miller, 1999; Reinke, 1998). The habit and practice of incorporating assessment as an integral part of learning experiences support the reflective process *when data are used to inform the process.*

The danger inherent in the shift to a focus on assessment seems to come from a view of accountability that values *testing* above all. In such a view, a single end-of-the-experience test, such as the FTCE or FCAT, because of the weight it carries, is all that matters in an instructional program. The force of a solitary test seems to guide every instructional decision. Well-intended, perhaps anxious, and even misguided personnel may actually mandate curricula for the sole purpose of teaching for one test. Such a response is actually the opposite of a standards-based model, as it completely misrepresents the intent of high-stakes tests, implies that the standards for learning are actually situated in one test, disregards the role of assessment, assumes that one test can accurately provide information about individual learning, and discounts the professional decision making of teachers (Cochran-Smith, 2005).

Contrary to a limited and linear view, the following model of standards-based teaching and learning (Figure 5.1) is more complex. In this model, assessment is part of the educative process and occurs throughout the experience, at least formally, for three purposes (to diagnose, monitor, and analyze results). Reflection, therefore, is represented by the arrows and by that which radiates in the various relationships between the star-shaped figures. Reflection is both process and product. In other words, reflective practitioners make connections between what they do to prepare for the product of student learning and what they do to monitor the process. The connections are possible because data exist to provide feedback to both teachers and learners.

As part of the assessment process, teachers shift to the role of researcher. They collect data, analyze their practice, test their assumptions, and discover what works in their own classroom, at one moment in time, with individual students, in one particular lesson.

Figure 5.1   Standards-based learning: A reflective model.

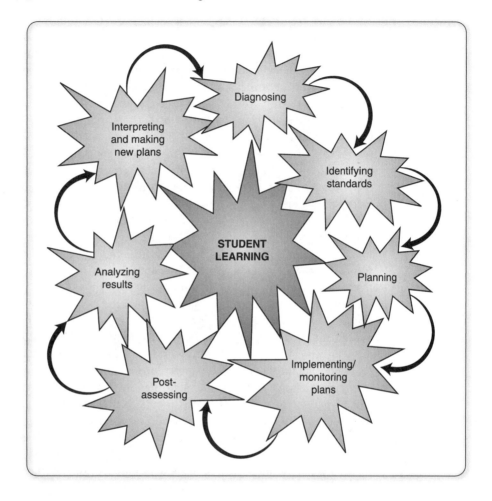

In this model, student learning is not only at the center, the result of sequenced planning and instruction, but it is also the core to which each part of the process connects. As teachers reflect on the context for their teaching, they do so with an eye on student learning outcomes; as they consider which standards to address, they think about the students with whom they will work; decisions about planning are based on what is needed to achieve desired results. Each step of the process is informed by student learning, just as it aims to impact learning gains for all students.

Informed decision making is evidence based (Cochran-Smith, 2005). It arises from a range of assessments conducted throughout the reflective process—before, during, and after teaching. As data are collected both formally and informally, they provide documented evidence of the learning experiences, enabling teachers to analyze and reflect on their work.

Seize the Data!

Rather than relying on scores from a solitary test, taken under extreme pressure at one point in a school year—a test not necessarily useful for teaching individual students—or rather than merely believing what students say about your teaching (they will "love" your lesson, "have fun," and "learn lots"), or rather than assuming that the failure of one detail means that you are a total teaching failure, collect data from multiple sources.

Actually, the high cost of large-scale assessments—in terms of money allocated but especially in terms of opportunities lost—is an argument for alternative assessments. Opportunities for reflection are lost if the only data collected are used at the end of a school year or the end of a lesson. One of the major differences in the new standards, compared to traditional tests of competency, is the move to change the nature of assessment, using more strategies for assessing learning, assessing authentic performances, and incorporating opportunities for peer and self-assessment (Heywood, 2000; Rankin, 1999).

Such assessments provide useful data throughout the learning process, thereby enhancing teaching and learning for teachers as well as students. Insights into the learning process are illuminated by analysis of data from multiple sources providing different perspectives, a chance to see better what is really going on. In his description of teacher action research, Richard Sagor (1992) argues for at least three windows for seeing, likened to studying life in a fish tank. If you gaze directly at the fish tank, writing a list of your observations, you may find 10 things in the tank. But in addition to four goldfish, three mollies, a castle, and two rocks, a view through the side of the tank may reveal a snail and a crab hiding behind the rocks; and a view from the top may show things floating on the water.

Choosing three windows or at least three sources of data, as opposed to scores from, say, one large-scale test, provides information that allows reflective teachers to know better what is happening in their classrooms. Such **triangulation** can take many forms in terms of methods for assessing individuals, some formal, some less formal, but the information gathered is interpreted in order to make formative decisions, supporting the learning process well before it ends.

Triangulation can happen in many ways. You can assess at three different points in the planning process: before you teach, during the lesson, and afterward to see what is retained, for example. You might even assess from the perspective of three different persons: the student's view, your view, and a peer's, parent's, or other teacher's view. You can also collect data from three learning domains on the student's knowledge (declarative), skill (procedural), and dispositions (affective). The important thing is to aim for reliable data, avoiding just one source of evidence to make visible student learning (see Articulating Your Stance).

Formative Assessment

Linking teaching more directly to student learning requires that teachers do business a bit differently than they may have been taught. For example, at the most practical level, we can shift the nature of classroom assessment from summative to formative. Lorrie Shepard (2000) compares the end-of-the-experience test (summative) to a medical screening conducted in a shopping mall, and she argues for in-depth, ongoing assessments of learning (**formative assessment**). Good formative assessment means that teachers must become

Like a researcher gazing into a fish tank, consider at least three ways you might study your own teaching.

1. Think of a lesson you once taught or designed. What are several kinds of data you might collect for assessment?
2. To triangulate your perspective on student learning, identify at least three data sources or windows for analysis.
3. Partner with a colleague. Discuss your plan for reflecting on the various assessments and data you will incorporate in your lesson.

more skilled as assessors, helping students learn how to keep their own records, monitor their own growth, and communicate their own learning using a variety of classroom-based assessment methods (Daniels & Bizar, 1998; Stiggins, 1999).

Think about your own ongoing professional development as you learn to be an effective teacher. In terms of your learning, the summative assessment, the FTCE assesses your teaching knowledge and skill. Can one test fairly determine your abilities as a teacher?

Fortunately, your learning can also be demonstrated through portfolios and other performance assessments. For example, both the National Board for Professional Teaching Standards (NBPTS) and the Interstate New Teacher Assessment and Support Consortium (INTASC) require teachers to include samples of student work *over time* as part of a portfolio assessment (Darling-Hammond, 1998, 1999).

The teacher work sample, another performance assessment designed to help teachers develop skill in standards-based teaching—especially in terms of multiple methods of assessment—can also be considered a formative assessment of teacher learning. Increasingly, work samples are valued for facilitating reflection on student learning (Wood, 2002).

If you have not yet experienced it, **teacher work sample methodology** is an applied performance that can be tailored to learning goals, teaching styles, group and individual student needs, and the context of the classroom, school, and community. At first glance, the work sample may look much like an extensive unit plan, but the differences are radical, akin to the reflective model of standards-based learning presented in Figure 5.2. Work sample methodology situates the teaching in a specific context and then utilizes data from pre- and postlesson and daily assessments to analyze the impact on learners.

Rather than present the knowledge of teachers (a traditional sample of their ability to plan) and rather than present the teachers' use of knowledge in practice (a traditional classroom observation by a university assessor), the work sample requires future teachers to describe the effect of their planning and instruction on PreK–12 students. More than just a planned unit of curriculum, a work sample documents the candidate's work; the students' work; the context and climate of the actual site where the unit was taught; the learning gains analyzed according to class, group, and individual results; and the preservice teacher's interpretation of the learning gains and reflection on the entire process (Wood, 2002).

The components of a work sample include a description of the setting, a rationale for the work sample topic, unit goals and objectives, lesson plans and materials, assessments aligned with the goals and objectives, analysis of student progress, an evaluative/interpretive essay, and a final reflective essay. The time frame for a teacher's work sample is typically 2 to 5 weeks, and so the focus is much like that of the real work of a classroom teacher on a specific period of teaching and learning. Teacher work sample methodology enables teachers to think about their emerging skills as assessors, especially (a) their ability to align goals, objectives, lessons, and assessments and (b) their ability to use assessment data to modify and adjust instruction for all students.

Teacher work sample methodology, recommended by NCATE (1999), is beginning to be implemented in teacher education programs nationwide. Data collected via work samples have the potential to document the learning gains of preservice teachers and to provide important feedback to the teacher education program. As instructional tools, work samples guide prospective teachers like yourself to connect *your* work to the learning gains of your students—*all* of your students. Work sample methodology represents what Robert Linn (2000) has called "a compelling case" for assessment "use that can improve education and student learning in dramatic ways." When fully understood, work sample methodology becomes a dynamic ongoing habit of mind visible in a teacher's classroom (Shepard, 2000).

Self-Assessment

Thoughtful, continuous assessment often includes a reflective component that encourages candidates to assess the impact of their teaching (Wood, 2002). In a review of the literature on methods for teachers to self-assess, Bullard (1998) identifies several formative approaches that support the growth of teachers: reflective evaluation, action research projects, teacher journals, techniques used to enhance teacher reflections on teaching, teaching portfolios, peer coaching, and several copyrighted programs.

Self-assessment has become an essential learning tool for students as well. In the shifting paradigm of *'learning'* and what it means in terms of the critical ability to perform in our increasingly complex society, self-direction, self-monitoring, and independent learning are essential skills. Effective teachers work *with* their students, using every possible method for shifting the responsibility for learning to the learner (see Articulating Your Stance).

ARTICULATING YOUR STANCE

1. What methods are you using to monitor and assess your own learning about how to be a teacher?
2. What evidence can you show to demonstrate your knowledge, skills, and dispositions?
3. What are some appropriate methods you will be able to use to help your students self-assess?

Reflections on Florida Standards: A Handbook for Teaching in the Sunshine State

What does it mean to be a reflective teacher? For one thing, it means that you have developed a professional identity; you know who you are and what you stand for. It also means that you understand that learning is a lifelong process, that you are never a finished product, and that you can continue to learn, in retrospect by reflecting-on-action, by reconsidering experience, even years after the fact. The ability to reflect means that you have also developed deliberative skill grounded in theory and research. You are courageous in the face of difficulty, and you have established yourself as an advocate for improving learning conditions so that all students reap benefits. As a reflective teacher, you are able to take informed positions.

As you know, educational policy is often a political decision and, as such, is potentially contentious. As social needs evolve, as the world grows increasingly complex, as technological advances reshape the workforce, as theories of teaching and learning are revised by ongoing research, and as best practices are determined according to contextual variables, debates within the profession are inevitable.

The intent of this book has been to offer a perspective on an essential issue, a hot topic in contemporary conversation. As part of the experience you are having as you finish reading this book, you are invited, mirror-like, to reflect on the process. In this section, I offer a lens for looking back.

Convention holds that authors usually introduce their purpose for writing a book in the preface or introduction at the beginning. For reasons that should be clear, I have resisted, until now, doing so. Assuming that you have read the first four chapters and have digested my suggestions for thinking intently about the link between teaching and learning, I now invite you to reconsider your views.

Keep in mind that this book has been written by a veteran classroom teacher, now a professor in a teacher education program in the state of Florida during a specific period of time. My hope is that as a reader, conscious of your own perspective, you are reading this book with an open mind, desiring to improve your own teaching practices. The knowledge and experience you bring to the text you alone know. You alone hold a vision for your own professional development and where you aim to go. Reading this book should inform your journey, so take what you can use.

Reflections on the First Four Chapters

This book has presented a framework for standards-based teaching, a model that puts student learning at the center. I have made the case that good lesson planning is not a set of enjoyable activities but a process of thinking about outcomes and how to achieve them. Planning requires a certain way of thinking, a habit of aligning standards, goals and objectives, learning events, and assessment to achieve the outcome you desire. Analysis of ongoing, purposeful assessment documents and informs the learning process, providing windows for seeing from multiple perspectives.

To help you understand your philosophy of teaching, I have threaded reflective prompts throughout the book. For example, the before-reading anticipation guides, Taking a Stance,

---

TAKING A STANCE REVISITED

To what degree do you agree or disagree with the following statements?

1. Holding teachers accountable for student learning is a bad idea and should not be done.
2. The job of the teacher is to provide good instruction, and the rest is up to students.
3. Standards get in the way of learning and limit what can be taught.
4. Teachers determine what students learn.
5. Writing formal lesson plans is akin to busy work; most teachers simply do not have time to do it.
6. It is critical that teachers treat all students equally.
7. Teachers should be hired because of their expertise in a content area. It is not their job to teach other subjects.
8. Effective teachers teach to the standards established for the subject and grade level at which they are hired to teach.
9. Research belongs in the ivory tower and is of little use in the practical work of classroom teaching.
10. I am (will be) a good teacher.

---

presented at the start of each chapter, were never intended to be answered definitively. In the Taking a Stance Revisited box above, you are invited to look back and reconsider selected questions that launched each of the four previous chapters. How has your thinking shifted?

Although I personally hold opinions about each statement, and even offered some fairly specific responses, explicit and implied, to the statements in each chapter, you need to form your own stance.

The boxed discussion questions, not at the start of each chapter but interspersed throughout the chapters, those under such as Informing Your Stance, also invited you to explore the issues addressed in each section in more detail. They represent another good dataset, an opportunity to now turn back, locating the discussion questions embedded in each of the previous chapters, reflecting, and responding personally, or possibly collaboratively with colleagues.

Reflections on the Lesson Plans

The sample lesson plans in Chapter 4, provide you with the opportunity to look at specific cases of standard-based teaching. The five lesson plans are entitled "Speak Up! Sharing Responsibility and Classroom Duties," "Listen and Learn: Memorizing the Parts of Speech!," "What a Concept! Analyzing Mathematical Thinking," "School Violence: A Critical Conversation," and "Discovering Theories about the Nature of Energy." No one lesson offers an ideal, but each contains features (Figure 5.2) that may seem appropriate or problematic, depending on the context.

The lessons address *Sunshine State Standards* in language arts, math, science, social studies, and health. In addition to content knowledge, the integrated lessons incorporate

Figure   5.2   Components of sample lesson plans.

Content Area	Grade Level	Literacy Skill	Delivery Model	Method of Assessment	Accommodation
Math	6th	Writing	Concept attainment	Holistic portfolio assessment	Gifted
Science	11th	Reading comprehension	Discovery	Attitudinal assessment	Alliterate
Social Studies	1st	Speaking	Problem solving	Analytic trait assessment	ESOL
Health	9th	Critical thinking	Collaborative groups	Peer assessment	Visually Impaired
Language Arts	3rd	Listening	Memory recall	Self-assessment	Behavior management

attention to literacy skill: reading comprehension, writing, speaking, listening, and critical thinking. Each lesson plan represents a different delivery model: lecture, discussion, collaborative groups, independent research, and reciprocal teaching. Each demonstrates accommodations for special needs students—gifted, alliterate, ESOL, visually impaired, and so on. Formal as well as informal assessments, each designed to appropriately match objectives, illustrate a range of possible ways to document student learning.

Guiding questions are provided in the next section of this chapter, by way of applied practice, to support either group discussion or personal reflection regarding the sample lesson plans. Questions are offered that are generic as well as located in specific aspects or plans.

In terms of specific plans, choose one of the sample lesson plans, located in Chapter 4, and discuss the questions in Articulating Your Stance.

ARTICULATING YOUR STANCE

1. Why did you choose this particular lesson?
2. What do you like about it?
3. In general, how well have the instructional materials been designed in terms of both what will be taught and how? If you were a substitute teacher handed this lesson plan, how successful would you be at implementing it?
4. What aspects do you anticipate might need changing? What changes do you suggest?
5. What other modifications can you suggest to support individual needs?
6. How might technology be integrated?
7. Imagine this lesson as part of a larger unit. What other goals and objectives would you address? What kinds of learning activities might you sequence before this lesson? What would you do after this lesson? What other methods of assessment would you include?

NFORMING YOUR STANCE

1. How well do the lesson plans identify what students are expected to learn? Do the goals and objectives align with the *Sunshine State Standards?*

2. Select an example of a learning outcome that seems especially clear, useful and verifiable. What makes this standard so strong?

3. Select an example of a learning outcome that should be restated for a clearer expectation of results.

4. Locate an assessment method that diagnoses student knowledge before teaching.

5. Locate an assessment that monitors progress during the lesson.

6. Locate an example of an assessment that evaluates a student's performance.

7. Locate an assessment that encourages self- or attitudinal assessment.

8. What lesson plan format, of the ones offered, do you prefer, and why?

9. In what aspects of the plans do you see echoes of methods, materials, or content from your own experiences in education? Are these positive or negative echoes?

While the specific lesson you chose to analyze may illustrate aspects of effective planning, this does not necessarily mean that the lesson will prove effective in any teaching context. As you continue to reflect on methods for modifying your instruction, never lose sight of how the success of chosen methods depends on context variables. Do not forget that the effectiveness of any lesson lies in the reflective ability of a teacher, a teacher who understands how to use assessment, ready to adjust for the needs of the targeted student population.

In terms of general principles, to review the features of effective planning and the habits of mind that seem to work best in standards-based instruction, revisit all five lesson plans in Chapter 4. Consider the guiding questions in Informing Your Stance as you discuss the quality of all five plans.

SUMMARY ≫

Now that you have read Chapter 5, and have completed the formative boxed exercises throughout the text, you have demonstrated increased knowledge, skill, and beliefs about the role of reflection and assessment in standards-based teaching and learning. As a final exercise, to show your increased understanding of the chapter's objectives, respond to the following short-answer questions:

1. Describe the role of reflection in the teaching and learning cycle.

2. Explain methods of self-assessment for teachers as well as students.

PREAMBLE TO CONTINUED READING ≫

One of the advantages of the teaching profession is that educators get to do it again, taking what they learn in one context and trying it again in a new context with new students and new methods. Experience is not always the best teacher, but the best teachers know how to learn from experience.

The best demonstration of your own reflection, at this point in your reading of this book, would be to stop and Extend Your Stance. Take time to write a three- to five-page statement of your philosophy of education. Define your beliefs about teaching and learning, and include a sharp focus on the role of assessment.

Reflective practitioners analyze the classroom experience using multiple methods. They interpret and apply the results, constantly improving their practice. In the day-to-day realities of the modern classroom, reflective teachers work hard to understand the results of their decisions, and they are careful about their assumptions. They resist efforts to micromanage or deskill their classroom practices by carefully testing their own effectiveness, analyzing data to determine what works best in the unique features of their classes (Goswami & Stillman, 1987; Sagor, 1992).

How will you know if you are a good teacher? The evidence will be in the work your students do and in the work you do reflecting on student evidence.

In Chapter 6, you will have the opportunity to think more about how to become more resourceful, considering the nature of collaboration and the local resources available to support your work and become more effective in your Florida classroom.

EXTENDING YOUR STANCE

Take time to draft a formal philosophy of education. Describe your beliefs, at this point in your professional development, about teaching and learning. Be sure to include your thoughts about effective instruction and the role of the teacher in impacting student learning gains.

Chapter 6

Collaboration

Goals and Objectives

After reading this chapter, readers will be able to:

I. Know more about teaching and learning in a standards-based system.
    6.1.1 Define collaborative partnerships.
    6.1.2 Describe national and state resources that support teaching and learning.

II. Monitor personal, professional development.
    6.2.1 Establish a network for personal, professional support.
    6.2.2 Craft new goals for ongoing professional development.

III. Refine personal philosophies for teaching and learning.
    6.3.1 Collaborate with key stakeholders.
    6.3.2 Advocate on behalf of all students.

Arguing for professional partnerships, this chapter provides resources to support teachers as they learn to thrive in a standards-based system.

No profession is as rewarding as teaching! Uncovering the rewards is especially easy when you engage in collegial relationships with those who share your passion, your enthusiasm, and your commitment. Take a few moments to consider the statements in the Taking a Stance box. Jot down your thoughts. Be sure to offer reasons and examples to explain your feelings.

How much voice you will have as a classroom teacher depends in part on the nature of the school in which you decide to work, but all teachers are largely curriculum planners. Will you have the necessary knowledge and skill to be an effective teacher?

TAKING A STANCE

To what extent do you agree or disagree with the following statements?

1. I worry that I will never know enough to be an effective teacher.
2. Decisions about teaching and learning are best made by experts such as district personnel, curriculum planners, educational researchers, and political policy makers.
3. When teachers have questions about their practice, they should consult a textbook or an administrator for help.

Teaching and Learning: A Team Effort

Setting standards, aligning assessments that measure what is taught, and providing high-quality, engaging instruction modified to support all learners will work if teachers are adequately prepared to do the work. The question of success ultimately rests with the quality of service provided to children. Therefore, resources to support the teaching and learning processes are critical.

No matter how well schooled teachers are, no matter how competent they feel, no matter how well they rank on licensure tests like the FTCE, one teacher alone cannot do the work, cannot know enough, cannot be enough, cannot give enough. Teaching and learning is a team sport and involves every teacher in the school (Goddard et al., 2004). Even the collective energy of the entire teaching faculty can be insufficient once the view of effectiveness shifts from teaching to learning. Leaving no child behind is a job requiring everyone's help.

In his synthesis of 35 years of research in effective schools, Marzano (2003) identified five factors that impact student learning: the school must have a guaranteed and viable curriculum, challenging goals and effective feedback, parental and community involvement, safe and orderly environment, and collegiality and professionalism. Without critical resources, Marzano's list of five school-level factors cannot be enacted, and no one teacher can manage so many important variables.

In order to "score high," supporting the success of every learner, the teaching-learning team must include players from the entire school building as well as from the extended community. Teachers should team with the students, each other, all staff and resource personnel, administrators, policy makers, parents, business leaders, and other partners. Together, the team agrees on the goals for each student, plans how to reach them, and utilizes all resources to get there (Brancarosa & Snow, 2004).

Learning to Trust Teachers

Teaching, as you know, is noble work. Quite possibly, no job is more critical to a nation's health and an individual's happiness. Yet, as a profession, teaching is often maligned (Moulthrop et al., 2005).

Historically, trusting the work of teachers has been an ongoing issue, perhaps as old a story as the history of formal education in the United States. From days in the past when teachers were always women and job requirements included wick trimming and no marriage allowed, to a job considered especially appropriate for mothers when their own children were at school, the public's perception of teachers has always been rather supercilious.

I graduated from Eastern Kentucky University with my degree in English Education and straight A's. In those days, Kentucky required a master's degree within 5 years for all teachers, and so I had remained in school, finishing both degrees. In the same number of years, my brother attained his bachelor's degree, with straight C's, but in engineering. That fall, my brother and I entered the job market at the same time. I accepted my first job teaching elementary school in the Kentucky mountains for $9,000 a year, and my brother was hired for his first job at $60,000. If you asked us today who has had the more rewarding career, even though his house has more guest rooms and my car has more miles, my smile would eclipse his.

Still, sadly, teachers have never had the same level of respect as members of other fields. This situation continues. In a recent best-seller, *Teachers Have It Easy: The Big Sacrifices and Small Salaries of America's Teachers,* the authors address current educational policies as a national scandal by presenting facts and figures outlining the difficult realities, including retention and recruitment. They compare the day in the life of a school teacher with that of a pharmaceutical sales representative, arguing for salary reform (Moulthrop et al., 2005).

It's true. As a professional educator in the 21st century, your salary will still be less than that of peers with equal education or teachers, say, in the state of Georgia. As you are hired in the current climate of acute shortages, you will find yourself teaching side by side with those who have even less training or respect than you. No matter how much we know, how long we study, or how high we score on tests of licensure, the public seems to believe that anyone can teach.

In the face of such opposition, especially in a society that places dollar values on everything, your self-esteem may suffer. Be careful not to believe society's perceptions and learn to respect the work you do. Equally, foster abiding respect for the work your colleagues do. Keep in mind that just as learners differ, so do teachers. Teaching collaboratively is a complicated act of relationship. Every member of the school team has a contribution to make. You are part of a joint effort, so please support all of those with whom you work.

Difficult for us all to accept is the fact that we can never know enough. As you develop your professional expertise as a teacher committed to student learning, you will continue to learn and grow. Remember what Samuel Johnson, the author of the *New English Dictionary* (now the *Oxford English Dictionary*), said about knowledge: it is less important to have knowledge of a thing than to know how to find the knowledge when it is necessary. If wisdom rests in knowing where to find help when you need it, then take time to uncover your resources. The best help will always come from other people, especially other teachers.

Rule one: avoid working alone. Seek the expertise of your colleagues, administrators, and community and professional resources (Hunter Quartz & the TEP Research Group,

2003). Join the teachers' union and other professional groups. Teachers who avoid judgments, who trust other teachers, who collaborate with their team, and who form professional affiliations are more likely to remain in the classroom, more likely to have a positive impact on their students, and more likely to grow in positions of teacher leadership. Collaboration, you will discover, can be one of the greatest joys of our profession (Goddard et al., 2004; Sagor, 1992).

Communicating with Stakeholders

If we are serious about improving the teaching and learning processes, determined to leave no child behind, then collaboration is essential. Under Florida's System of School Improvement and Accountability, every public school in the state must have a School Advisory Council (SAC). Membership of the local council includes parents and members from the community, as well as teachers, administrators, and support staff from the school. It is the job of the council to develop plans for improving teaching and learning for a particular school (DelMonte, 2002).

Parents must be part of the process, as should the community at large. Accountability, in this vision, works both ways. Just as educators must demand the resources necessary to do the work, we must understand the community's right to expect results (Swope & Miner, 2000).

Sometimes, when we are questioned about our decisions, we feel defensive, especially if we are already suffering from insecurity. During my first year as a teacher (the year of the $9,000 salary), I found myself overwhelmed in a self-contained fourth-grade classroom. I worked hard to design engaging lessons for my 38 students, using all I knew about best practices, and the children seemed to love my class. But the school was in a small rural town, and I was an outsider in the community.

Every afternoon, before the final bell, I would glance out of my classroom's second-floor window and notice parents in the parking lot waiting to pick up their children. Obviously, they were flocking together, talking about me. I just knew they thought I was doing a terrible job, and I did not know what to do. As my insecurities grew, I desperately sought better ways to engage the students. Field trips, guest speakers, active learning—my methods were varied. Still, the parking lot whispers continued.

Fortunately, one of the mothers had been a teacher. During the first parent conference, she kindly explained my problem. "You see," she said, "you are doing too much with the students. Parents listen as their children talk about all the fun they had at school, and they are jealous. Because you keep the kids so busy during the day, they carry their books home at night. We feel as if we're being the teacher!"

She was right. I had been so intent on "active learning" that I had neglected time for independent work at school. At the end of the day, I had not even noticed the poor children laboring out the door with backpacks weighed down by piles of heavy books! I had been too worried about what the parents thought about *me*.

Kristin Mudd, a first-year teacher in Duvall County, reported a similar problem with parents, one she tackled early in her career by facing it head on. "My age seemed to muffle

Figure 6.1   Working with parents.

For teacher Chuck Glaeser, parent conferences take place in the media center at a round table. He prepares for such conferences with the end in mind. "I envision the parent walking out, shaking my hand, smiling, and thanking me for the good job I'm doing."

Chuck dresses professionally, wearing a tie and a sport coat. He brings documentation of the student's work, a small pad, and a business card.

When a parent asks, "How is my child doing in your class?" Chuck responds with his own question: "Aside from her grade, how do you think she's doing? What do you notice about her at home that might tell you how she's doing?" If the student is present, he asks her to give her impressions as well.

Chuck lists specific student strengths, and he provides examples. After a positive start, he addresses the targeted needs or problem. He does that by asking the student, "What's the next step we need to take?"

Together, Chuck, the parent, and, hopefully, the student map out a three- or four-step plan on Chuck's notepad. The plan goes home with the parent. Chuck shakes hands, smiles, and says, "Thank *you.*"

By permission from Chuck Glaeser.

my confidence with parents since day one. Only lately have I decided to conquer this problem and thus have become a frequent parent caller."

Kristin calls parents "at the first sign of trouble" and when students experience outstanding achievement. She phones to praise, complain, and listen. "Speaking with the parent," she says "explains worlds about the chld." According to Kristin's developing expertise, "More times than not, parents are willing to support your decisions and reinforce your efforts. The challenge is to keep the lines of communication open."*

Veteran high school teacher Chuck Glaeser, from Orlando, agrees. "I began teaching at a private school where parents were heavily involved. Though the formal parent-teacher conference existed, my interactions with parents took place much more frequently in the hallways between classes, on the football field, at the homecoming dance, and at students' houses for dinner and parties."† Chuck likens his early interactions with parents to "a kind of boot camp" in which he was able to learn some important skills (Figure 6.1).

Chuck Glaeser believes that his success with parents results from his personal teaching philosophy. "I think very highly of the work I do," he says, "and because I take teaching seriously and believe I do my job well, I never go into a parent conference feeling that I have anything to prove or anything to defend. I know it's not about me; it's about the parent and child. I feel that all I have to do is try to befriend them, to let them know that we can work together."

*By permission from Kristin Mudd.
†By permission from Chuck Glaeser.

Chuck understands that working with parents is a critical part of his job, and he tries to learn all he can from the conference. "As a private school teacher," he explains, "I knew that I was working for the parents who paid my salary. I feel very much the same way now as a public school teacher. But it's not about them paying my salary; it's about me being a servant to the citizens of my community, who include the parents of my students."[‡]

Accountability involves all members of the school team as well as students and parents. The multiple perspectives of all who have a stake in student learning can feel burdensome, even frightening. Input from others can also provide important information that can help you as a teacher do your job better.

Rule two: listen to the questions and complaints against you. If you give a writing assignment, for example, and students raise their hands to ask, "How long does it have to be?" you probably need to rethink your directions. Questions from others (particularly those who, like parents and students, care about successful learning) are a source of data that will provide insight. Attend carefully, consider all perspectives, and make the best decisions you can. Careful listening is one way you will learn from experience and grow (see Articulating Your Stance).

Professional Credibility

For all the bright and talented teachers who thrive, there are others who become discouraged by the difficult challenges; they burn out and leave the profession (Hunter Quartz & the TEP Research Group, 2003). Do not let that happen to you. Developing professional fortitude and the requisite expertise to be an effective teacher takes time. Your continued professional development is one of your primary responsibilities.

Credibility as a teacher takes time to establish. It comes from many sources. Perhaps you are unusually mature or a parent yourself. Possibly you are highly knowledgeable in a content area. Maybe your degree or licensure training came from an institution

---

ARTICULATING YOUR STANCE

Take a few minutes to write reflectively.

1. Think of your family, friends, and loved ones. Do they value your choice of a profession? How do you know? How do you feel about their views of your choice?

2. As a teaching novice, make a list of all the fears that haunt you. Pinpoint your key worries and then add a postscript to each. Why do you think these aspects of teaching are so worrisome?

3. Identify the colleagues, friends, resources, and informants you will recruit to help you meet the challenges. Share your reflection with one of those marvelous supporters when you are done!

[‡]By permission from Chuck Glaeser.

respected in the field. You might have interned or served as a substitute teacher, so word of your work preceded you. But for most beginning teachers, unknown in a new place, the first few years are about establishing yourself and becoming reputable.

If you can assume full responsibility, not for being *liked* but for caring about every child's success, you will quickly earn the respect of those with whom you work. As you shift your worries from yourself to your students, you will discover that the nature of the difficulty shifts too. Suddenly, it becomes more important to talk with colleagues, not about what others might be saying about you, but about how best to help solve teaching and learning problems. Use your resources, and your credibility will skyrocket.

Two national organizations dedicated to issues of teaching and learning are the National Education Association (NEA) and the American Federation of Teachers. Most states have state affiliates as well. For example, in Florida, the Florida Education Association is a state chapter of the NEA. In some states, such as Ohio or New York, you automatically become a member of a teachers' union once you sign a job contract. But Florida, like Texas and North Carolina, prohibits union members from bargaining, and you have to sign up to become a member (Walters, 2004).

Important for your ongoing professional career, in addition to tapping the human resources in your school, district, and community, professional resources, both organizations and information, are just a click away. The next best suggestion for defining terms and finding resources on any topic is to explore the search capabilities of the Internet.

Learned Societies

A selective list of professional organizations is presented here as a resource. Listed in alphabetical order, these learned societies have either been discussed elsewhere in the book or have potential value for readers. Many such groups exist, and most are excellent sources for locating national standards.

In addition, professional organizations host annual meetings, open for teachers, featuring the latest teaching methods, research, and practices. The Web sites of these organizations offer vast resources in terms of position statements on educational issues, publications to support teachers' work, and further contacts regarding membership benefits. Support your ongoing professional development by joining at least one organization whose membership will inform your teaching.

American Alliance for Health, Physical Education, Recreation and Dance (AAHPERD)
http://www.aahperd.org

American Association of Colleges for Teacher Education (AACTE) *http://aacte.org*

American Educational Research Association (AERA) *http://www.aera.net*

Association of Teacher Educators (ATE) *http://www.ate.1.org*

International Reading Association (IRA) *http://www.reading.org*

International Society for Technology in Education (ISTE) *http://www.iste.org*

International Technology Association (ITA) *http://www.iteawww.org*

Interstate New Teacher Assessment and Support Consortium (INTASC) *http://www.ccsso.org/project*

Music Teachers National Association (MTNA) *http://www.mtna.org*

National Art Education Association (NAEA) *http://www.naea-reston.org*

National Association for the Education of Young Children (NAEYC) *http://www.naeyc.org*

National Association for Multicultural Education (NAME) *http://www.nameorg.org*

National Association of Special Education Teachers (NASET) *http://www.naset.org*

National Association of State Directors of Teacher Education and Certification (NASDTEC)
   http://www.nasdtec.org

National Board for Professional Teaching Standards (NBPS) *http://www.nbpts.org*

National Council for Accreditation of Teacher Education (NCATE) *http://www.ncate.org*

National Council for the Social Studies (NCSS) *http://www.socialstudies.org*

National Council of Teachers of English (NCTE) *http://www.ncte.org*

National Council of Teachers of Math (NCTM) *http://www.nctm.org*

National Dance Education Organization (NDEO) *http://www.ndeo.org*

National Middle School Association (NMSA) *http://www.nctm.org*

National Science Teachers Association (NSTA) *http://www.nsta.org*

Professional Bibliography

The national organizations listed above also offer publications of particular use to teachers and others interested in curriculum design. Most learned societies often host professional development conferences in scenic Florida. Whenever possible, attend professional meetings. You will discover that they are a secret of professional longevity, a veritable fountain of inspiration.

Print resources will support your continued professional development as well. The following bibliography is a partial list of books, journals, and Web sites especially useful for helping educators connect teaching to learning.

Books

Danielson, C. (1996). *Enhancing professional practice: A framework for teaching.* Alexandria, VA: Association for Supervision and Curriculum Development.

Freiberg, H. J., & Driscoll, A. (2005). *Universal teaching strategies.* Boston: Pearson.

Gardner, H. (1999). *Intelligence reframed: Multiple intelligences for the twenty-first century.* New York: Basic Books.

Gunter, M. A., Estes, T. H., & Schwab, J. (1999). *Instruction: A models approach.* Boston: Allyn & Bacon.

Herrell, A. L. (2000). *Fifty strategies for teaching English language learners.* Upper Saddle River, NJ: Merrill.

Hurt, J. (2003). *Taming the standards: A commonsense approach to higher student achievement, K–12.* Portsmouth, NH: Heinemann.

Kottler, E., Kottler, J. A., & Kottler, C. J. (1998). *Secrets for secondary school teachers: How to succeed in your first year.* Thousand Oaks, CA: Corwin Press.

McMillan, J. H. (2001). *Classroom assessment: Principles and practice for effective teaching.* Boston: Allyn & Bacon.

Olson, S., & Loucks-Horsley, S. (2000). *Inquiry and the National Science Education Standards: A guide for teaching and learning.* Committee on the Development of an Addendum to the National Science Education Standards on Scientific Inquiry. Washington, DC: National Research Council.

Popham, W. J. (1999). *Classroom assessment: What teachers need to know.* Boston: Allyn & Bacon.

Weber, E. (2005). *MI strategies in the classroom and beyond: Using roundtable learning.* Boston: Pearson.

Wiggins, G., & McTighe, J. (1998). *Understanding by design.* Alexandria, VA: Association for Supervision and Curriculum Development.

Zemelman, S., Daniels, H., & Hyde, A. (1998). *Best practice: New standards for teaching and learning in America's schools.* Portsmouth, NH: Heinemann.

Journals

American Journal of Health Education Covers today's health education and health promotion issues head on with timely, substantive, and thought-provoking articles. *http://www.aahperd.org/aahe/template.cfm?template=ajhe_main.html*

Community Outreach and Education for the Arts Handbook A handbook for promoting music and the other arts in our schools and communities. *http://www.mtna.org/pubs.htm*

English Journal Contains ideas for English language arts teachers in middle and high schools. Each issue examines the relationship of theory and research to classroom practice and reviews current materials of interest to English teachers, including books and electronic media. *http://www.ncte.org/pubs/journals/ej*

Journal of Adolescent & Adult Literacy Offers practical classroom-tested ideas grounded in sound research and theory. Whether you work with new or struggling readers, or with students who are skilled in reading and writing, you'll find something of interest in *JAAL.* *http://www.reading.org/publications/journals/jaal/index.html*

Journal of Dance Education Publishes original articles on topics and issues related to the practical and theoretical aspects of dance education and training of dancers, curriculum, policy, advocacy, technology, safety, and teaching process, methodology, and certification/licensure. *http://www.ndeo.org/publications.asp#jode*

Language Arts Provides a forum for discussions on all aspects of language arts learning and teaching, primarily as they relate to children in prekindergarten through the eighth grade. *http://www.ncte.org/pubs/journals/la*

Learning & Leading with Technology Features practical, usable ideas for improving educational outcomes with technology. *http://www.iste.org/Template.cfm?Section=Publications&Template=/TaggedPage/TaggedPageDisplay.cfm&TPLID=15&ContentID=4448*

Mathematics Teacher (MT) Monthly journal for high school teachers that offers activities, lesson ideas, teaching strategies, and problems through in-depth articles, departments, and features. *http://my.nctm.org/eresources/journalhome.asp?journalid=2*

Mathematics Teaching in the Middle School (MTMS) Monthly journal for middle school teachers that offers activities, lesson ideas, teaching strategies, and problems through in-depth articles, departments, and features. *http://my.nctm.org/eresources/journalhome.asp?journalid=3*

Middle Ground Provides a voice and a resource for those committed to the educational and developmental needs of young adolescents. *http://www.nmsa.org/Publications/MiddleGround/tabid/437/Default.aspx*

Middle Level Learning Brings together lesson ideas and theoretical content focused on the middle grades. *http://www.socialstudies.org/publications/mll*

Middle School Journal Contains articles that promote middle-level education and contribute to an understanding of the educational and developmental needs of youth between the ages of 10 and 15. *http://www.nmsa.org/Publications/MiddleSchoolJournal/tabid/435/Default.aspx*

Multicultural Perspectives Each edition includes feature articles, reviews, program descriptions, and other pieces by and for multicultural educators and activists around the world. *http://www.nameorg.org/publications.html*

Science & Children NSTA's professional journal for elementary school teachers. Topics include assessment, technological applications, activities, and inquiry. *http://www.nsta.org/elementaryschool#journal*

Science Scope NSTA's professional journal for middle school teachers. Topics include assessment, technological applications, activities, and inquiry. *http://www.nsta.org/middleschool#journal*

The Science Teacher NSTA's professional journal for high school teachers. Topics include assessment, technological applications, activities, and inquiry. *http://www.nsta.org/highschool#journal*

Social Education Includes techniques for using teaching materials in the classroom, information on the latest instructional technology, reviews of educational media, research on significant topics related to social studies, and lesson plans that can be applied to various disciplines. *http://www.socialstudies.org/publications/se*

Social Studies and the Young Learner Presents teaching techniques designed to stimulate the reading, writing, and critical thinking skills vital to classroom success. *http://www.socialstudies.org/publications/ssyl*

The Special Educator E-Journal This electronic journal contains all the latest information to be found on the Internet concerning the field of teaching exceptional children. *http://www.naset.org/publications.0.html*

Strategies: A Journal for Physical and Sport Educators Bimonthly journal that delivers practical ideas, how-to information, and tips for sport and physical educators. *http://www.aahperd.org/naspe/template.cfm?template=strategies_main.html*

Teaching Children Mathematics (TCM) Monthly journal for elementary school teachers that offers activities, lesson ideas, teaching strategies, and problems through in-depth articles, departments, and features. *http://my.nctm.org/eresources/journalhome.asp?journalid=4*

The Technology Teacher Content includes reports of current trends in technology education, technology learning activities, program articles, news, and a calendar for the elementary, middle, and high school teacher. *http://www.iteaconnect.org/F1.html*

Voices from the Middle Each issue includes teachers' descriptions of authentic classroom practices, middle school students' reviews of adolescent literature, a technology column, and reviews of professional resources for teachers. *http://www.ncte.org/pubs/journals/vm*

YC (Young Children) This practitioner-based journal devotes special attention to issues in the field of early childhood education. *http://www.journal.naeyc.org/*

Web Sites

LESSON PLANS

Blue Web'n

Online library of *handpicked* Internet sites categorized by subject, grade level, and format (tools, references, lessons, hotlists, resources, tutorials, activities, projects). *http://www.kn.sbc.com/wired/bluewebn/search.cfm*

Educator's Reference Desk

Over 2,000 free lesson plans organized by academic department and grade level. *http://www.eduref.org/Virtual/Lessons/index.shtml*

Kathy Schrock's Guide for Educators

Lesson plans organized by academic department and elementary/middle/high school levels. *http://school.discovery.com/lessonplans*

LessonPlansPage.com

Over 2,500 free lesson plans organized by academic department and grade level. *http://www.lessonplanspage.com*

LessonPlanz.com

Free lesson plans organized by academic department and grade level. *http://www.lessonplanz.com/*

Teachers.Net

Lesson plans organized by academic department and elementary/middle/high school levels. *http://www.teachers.net/cgi-bin/lessons/sort.cgi?searchterm=Literature*

INTEGRATING TECHNOLOGY

Strategies for Integrating Technology into Your Curriculum

Helpful technology-related Web sites organized by topic (dialogue with experts, publishing projects, multimedia resources, and more). *http://www.gp.k12.mi.us/ci/ce/computer/strategies.htm*

Technology Curriculum Integration Ideas

Browse technology ideas by academic department. *http://www.remc11.k12.mi.us/bcisd/classres/intideas.htm#english*

The Webquest Page

Offers general information about Web quests. Also, search examples of Web quests by subject and grade level. *http://webquest.sdsu.edu/webquest.html*

ASSESSMENT

Authentic Assessment

A *handpicked* index of authentic assessment resources. *http://www.uwstout.edu/soe/profdev/assess.shtml*

Authentic Assessment Toolbox
> Information about authentic assessment as well as examples organized by academic department. *http://jonathan.mueller.faculty.noctrl.edu/toolbox/index.htm*

Kathy Schrock's Guide for Educators
> Provides hundreds of general and subject-specific rubrics. *http://school.discovery.com/schrockguide/assess.html#rubrics*

ART EDUCATION WEB SITES

Art Education Page for K12
> Offers art-related Web resources organized by art history, art museums, lesson plans, journals, organizations, and much more. *http://falcon.jmu.edu/~ramseyil/arteducation.htm#E*

Artsonia
> Student art gallery that showcases school art projects from around the world. *http://www.artsonia.com*

Crayola
> Provides art lesson plans by topic, grade, time frame, and theme. Also offers art techniques and a gallery of student work. *http://www.crayola.com/*

HEALTH EDUCATION WEB SITES

PBS Teacher Source
> Provides lesson plans and activities categorized by topic and grade level. *http://www.pbs.org/teachersource/health.htm*

PE Central
> Offers health lesson ideas categorized by topic (diseases, personal health, nutrition, etc.). *http://www.pecentral.org/lessonideas/health/healthlp.asp*

Selected, High Quality Teacher-Tested Resources for PK–16 Educators
> Health-related lesson ideas and resources organized by topic, resource type, or grade level. *http://www.ideas.wisconsin.edu/subject.cfm?sid=42*

LANGUAGE ARTS EDUCATION WEB SITES

Awesome Library
> Lesson plans organized by topic and grade level. *http://www.awesomelibrary.org/Library/MaterialsSearch/LessonPlans/LanguageArts.html*

Outta Ray's Head
> A collection of lesson plans and handouts categorized by literature, writing, and poetry. *http://home.cogeco.ca/~rayser3/lessons3.htm*

Web English Teacher
> Lesson plans and helpful Web sites organized by topic (writing, grammar, authors, poets, and much more). *http://www.webenglishteacher.com/*

MATH EDUCATION WEB SITES

Math Forum
> Guide to selected Web sites on several dozen math topics from basic operations to vectors. *http://mathforum.org/library/topics/*

Math Forum Library
> Search for math-related Web sites by grade level, resource type (games, organization, software, field trips, and many more), and topic (arithmetic, algebra, geometry, and many more). *http://mathforum.org/library/topics/*

Mid-Continent Research for Education and Learning
> Math lesson plans organized by topic as well as a long list of additional resources. *http://www.mcrel.org/lesson-plans/math/mathlessons.asp*

MUSIC EDUCATION WEB SITES

K–12 Resources for Music Educators
> Carefully researched resources for music educators and students in all areas and at all educational levels. *http://www.isd77.k12.mn.us/resources/staffpages/shirk/k12.music.html*

Instructional Materials in Music
> Lists helpful Web sites for music teachers from teaching ideas to teaching tools. *http://www.cln.org/subjects/musicinst.html*

The Music Teacher's Resource Site
> Offers a variety of activities and musical arrangements. *http://www.mtrs.co.uk/arrange.htm*

PHYSICAL EDUCATION WEB SITES

PE Central
> Offers PE lesson plans categorized by grade level, as well as assessment and classroom management activities. *http://www.pecentral.org/lessonideas/searchlessonideas.asp*

PE Links 4 U: Promoting Active & Healthy Lifestyles
> Contains PE-related editorials, the latest news, lesson ideas, and more. *http://www.pelinks4u.org/*

Physical Education Lesson Plan Page
> View a variety of lesson ideas submitted by other physical educators. *http://members.tripod.com/~pazz/lesson.html*

READING EDUCATION WEB SITES

RAMP to Reading Resources
> Online resources about reading instruction, book talks, reading incentive programs, graphic organizers for reading, book lists, and much more. *http://richmond.k12.va.us/readamillion/readingresources.htm*

Teachnology
> Lists a variety of reading lesson ideas. *http://www.teach-nology.com/teachers/lessonplans/language arts/reading*

The Teachers' Corner
> Reading lesson ideas and resources arranged by genre, parts of speech, phonics, reading skills, spelling, vocabulary, and much more. *http://www.theteacherscorner.net/reading*

SCIENCE EDUCATION WEB SITES

Frank Potter's Science Gems
> Over 14,000 science resources organized by category, subcategory, and grade level. *http://www.sciencegems.com*

Science NetLinks
> Lessons, tools, and resources organized by topic and grade level.
> *http://www.sciencenetlinks.com/tool_index.cfm*

Scope, Sequence, and Coordination
> Micro-units that include both student and teacher materials. *http://dev.nsta.org/ssc*

SOCIAL STUDIES EDUCATION WEB SITES

Awesome Library
> Access to resources and lesson plans organized by categories, including biographies, current events, multicultural, and more. *http://www.awesomelibrary.org/social.html*

Organization for Community Networks
> Wide variety of lesson plans organized by grade. *http://ofcn.org/cyber.serv/academy/ace*

Social Studies School Service
> Resources and lesson ideas organized by topic and grade. *http://socialstudies.com*

SPECIAL EDUCATION WEB SITES

American Teachers
> Dedicated to improving the education and lives of students and loved ones with exceptionalities and disabilities, as well as the gifted. Offers lesson plans as well as resources for a variety of special education topics. *http://www.americanteachers.com/specialed.cfm*

Gifted Education and Special Education Lesson Plans and Resources
> Lesson plans and resources organized by ability types.
> *http://www.cloudnet.com/~edrbsass/edexc.htm*

Kodak Lesson Plans
> Using photography in the special education classroom.
> *http://www.kodak.com/global/en/consumer/education/lessonPlans/indices/specialEducation.shtml*

Florida Resources

In Florida, many resources exist to support effective teaching. This section includes a partial list of helpful Web sites and contact information for the Florida Department of Education and other state organizations.

Florida Department of Education

Because so much is likely to change annually, the Florida Department of Education is one of the best resources for finding the latest information about the state's standards and assessment practices.

From the main Web site, *http://www.fldoe.org*, following the links for educators' resources, teachers can find an abundance of helpful information.

An excellent resource for helping you prepare for the FTCE exam, *Competencies and Skills Required for Teacher Certification in Florida, Ninth Edition* is available at the Bureau of Educator Certification (*http://www.firn.edu/doe/dpe/publications.htm*).

To support your efforts to stay informed regarding the FCAT, the FCAT Test Development Center in the Division of Assessment and School Performance at the Department of Education offers a host of FCAT products and publications. All of the following are available at *http://www.firn.edu/doe/sas/fcat.htm*:

About the FCAT Web Brochure

This Web-based version of the Parent Brochure is located on the Department of Education Web site and is available in English, Spanish, and Haitian Creole.

Assessment & Accountability Briefing Book

This book provides an overview of Florida's assessment, school accountability, and teacher certification programs. FCAT topics include frequently asked questions, content assessed by the FCAT, reliability, and validity. The booklet can be downloaded from the Department of Education Web site.

FCAT Committees

An annual report of school district participation in the development, design, review, and scoring of the FCAT is sent to superintendents each August. Along with this report is a request for new nominations for the FCAT committee member database.

FCAT Handbook—A Resource for Educators

This document for educators and administrators provides comprehensive information about the FCAT program. It includes information about the test development process, the design of the tests, the scoring of the tests, and other information of interest to public educators and policy makers.

FCAT Myths vs. Facts

This brochure provides factual information about the FCAT program by addressing common concerns about the FCAT based on myths.

FCAT Performance Task Scoring—Practice for Educators (publications and software)

These materials are designed to help teachers learn to score FCAT reading, writing, and mathematics performance tasks at Grades 4, 5, 8, and 10. A Trainer's Guide includes instructions for using the scoring publications and software in teacher education seminars and workshops. The publications mirror the scorer training experiences by presenting samples of student work for teachers to score.

FCAT Posters

The colorful 17 by 23 inch elementary, middle, and high school FCAT reading, writing, science, and mathematics posters have an instructional focus and are available at district assessment offices. A high school poster provides information to students about the graduation requirement to pass the FCAT reading and mathematics tests and about the multiple opportunities available to retake the tests.

FCAT Test Item Specifications

Defining both the content and the format of the FCAT test questions, the Specifications primarily serve as guidelines for FCAT test item writers and reviewers but also contain information for educators and the general public.

Florida Reads! Florida Solves! Florida Writes! and Florida Inquires!

Each grade and subject-level publication provides information about FCAT scoring.

Frequently Asked Questions about FCAT

This brochure provides answers to frequently asked questions about the FCAT program.

Keys to FCAT

These booklets are distributed each January and contain information for parents and students preparing for the FCAT test.

Lessons Learned—FCAT, Sunshine State Standards and Instructional Implications

This document provides an analysis of previous years' FCAT results and contains analyses of state FCAT data through 2000. The analysis may assist educators in interpreting and understanding their local FCAT scores, which could help improve instruction in the classroom.

Parent Brochure

This colorful foldout brochure for parents provides information about FCAT reading, writing, mathematics, and science for Grades 3–10. It is designed to provide an overview as well as detailed information across grades and subject areas. Brochure in English, Spanish, and Haitian Creole are available, upon request, from the Department of Education.

Sample Test Materials for the FCAT

These materials are produced and distributed each fall for teachers to use with students. The students' booklet contains a list of the different kinds of FCAT questions, practice questions, and hints for answering them. The teacher's answer key provides the correct answers and an explanation for the correct answers, and also indicates which *Sunshine State Standards* benchmark is being assessed by each question.

The New FCAT NRT: Stanford Achievement Test, Tenth Edition

This brochure outlines differences between the previous FCAT norm-referenced test (SAT) and the current FCAT NRT (SAT10).

Understanding FCAT Reports

This booklet provides information about the student, district, and school reports for the recent test administration. Samples of reports, explanations of the reports, and a glossary of technical terms are included. Distribution to districts is scheduled to coincide with the delivery of student reports each May.

What Every Teacher Should Know About FCAT

This document provides suggestions for all subject area teachers to use in helping their students succeed on the FCAT. Like most of the publications listed here, it can be downloaded from the Department of Education Web site.

State Organizations

In addition to the Florida Department of Education, other state organizations provide materials, information, and resources free of charge. In your ongoing efforts to garner all the support you can, never hesitate to contact agencies, institutions, and other concerned groups. This section includes a partial list of helpful Web sites and contact information for a few state organizations.

- *Assistive Technology Education Network (ATEN).* Headquartered in Sanford, ATEN has resource and demonstration labs in areas across Florida that can loan and train educators on technological tools to assist students with special technology.

- *Florida Association for Supervision and Curriculum Development (FASCD).* FASCD publishes *Florida Educational Leadership,* a journal dedicated to improving K–12 education in Florida.

- *The Florida Educational Technology Conference (http://www.fetc.org),* usually held in January, provides a forum for teachers and other educators to keep abreast of technological advances. For over 25 years, this meeting has offered workshops, presentations, exhibits, and demonstrations, with people from all over the country exchanging the latest innovations as well as classroom practices.

- *Local Assistive Technology Specials (LATS).* Each county in Florida has a network of local professionals to support students with special needs.

- Most national organizations have state affiliates, and these can be found by contacting the national organization for information. For example, the Florida Council of Teachers of English is an affiliate of the National Council of Teachers of English, and the Florida Reading Association is a state affiliate of the International Reading Association.

- *Regional Florida Diagnostic and Learning Resources System (FDLRS) Centers.* These centers provide regional support for assistive technology to support students with disabilities.

- Florida offers National Writing Project summer institutes for teachers of any discipline or grade level interested in developing their abilities as teachers of writing. For more information, contact one of the state's writing project Web sites:

Florida State University Writing Project 850-644-1909
http://www.esp.fsu.edu/dwyerweb/fsuwp/firstpage.html

National Writing Project at Florida Gulf Coast University 239-590-7808
http://coe.fgcu.edu/fgcwp

National Writing Project at the University of Central Florida 407-823-3405
http://www.nwpucf.org

South Florida Writing Project 954-262-8633 *http://www.schoolofed.nova.edu/sfwp*

Tampa Bay Area Writing Project 813-974-7310 *http://www.coedu.usf.edu/tbawp*

R ESEARCHING YOUR STANCE

1. Choose and investigate some of the resources listed in this chapter that seem potentially relevant to your professional goals. Report on what you find.

2. Be sure to include at least one Web site from a professional organization that fits your teaching aspirations. Summarize the site, noting the contents and topics addressed.

3. Focusing on what you can use, what do you find helpful? Why?

SUMMARY »

This chapter was designed to help you think about your teaching role within a broader context. Sometimes even the most talented and experienced teachers allow their perceived limitations or inadequacies to get the best of them. Rather than isolate yourself, be resourceful! Become part of an educational team and recruit all concerned parties to collaborate. Professional partnerships can provide countless resources to support your efforts to help all students succeed.

In a final written reflection, as evidence that you have mastered the objectives of this chapter, take time to:

1. Describe the characteristics of collaborative partnerships.
2. List some national and state resources that you expect will support your professional efforts.
3. Describe five or more personal resources that you intend to utilize to ensure your personal and professional support.
4. Draft a brief statement outlining steps you will take to ensure that all students make sustained, regular progress.

Extending Your Stance offers suggestions concerning activities for further reflection about the teaching-learning connection in the current age of accountability.

In Chapter 1, I stated that teachers interested in fostering a clearer connection between the plans they make, the lessons they teach, and, ultimately, the gains their students make face a three-pronged challenge. Teachers must know (a) how to target *appropriate* standards, thereby determining the goals and objectives they want students to learn; (b) how to design lessons that result in high levels of student learning; and (c) in the end,

---

EXTENDING YOUR STANCE

1. Interview a classroom teacher. You might ask:
   - With whom do you collaborate?
   - What personal and professional resources sustain you?
   - How has your understanding of what it means to work with parents changed?
2. If you can spend some time in a classroom or as a visitor in a school, explore the policies for identifying student needs, for methods of collaborative action, and for resources to accommodate special teaching and learning challenges.
3. Compare your answers with those of other interviewers. What patterns emerge? For example, in the responses of teachers, in what ways, if any, does length of experience matter?
4. Continue to gather professional resources, including Internet sites, specialized organizations, and other human and material means for achieving excellent results, becoming a teacher who makes a difference.

how to demonstrate— to students, parents, principals, other interested participants, and themselves—that they made a difference in the learning and lives of all students, including those with learning disabilities, language barriers, and other special needs.

As you buy new school clothes, sharpen your pencils, gather your books, and prepare to enter a classroom on the other side of the desk, continue to be patient with you own learning. Do not lose sight of your target—student learning—but set reasonable goals for yourself and find the resources to achieve them. Remember, the process of effective teaching and learning is in part a slow-growth model. But with increasing knowledge, steady effort, strong mentoring, careful reflection, and time to develop your skills, you will find your way to help your students find theirs.

PREAMBLE TO CONTINUED THINKING ≫

How do teachers at all levels link teaching to learning? Perhaps the first step is to agree that student learning is the ultimate goal of teaching and that the primary role of teachers is to assume responsibility for the results of our practice. We need to believe that all students can achieve; we need to value what students bring to the classroom; and we need to care enough about student progress to advocate for necessary resources, for equity, and for attention to students' emotional and social growth (Cochran-Smith, 2005).

Focusing more sharply on learning to make it more explicit can happen in several ways. For example, in day-to-day conversation, we can stop using the word *teaching* and substitute *learning*. Teaching is one way to get to learning. As we talk often about student learning, we can tell our students directly, "My goal is to help you learn to read better, solve problems, or think like a historian." By action, word, and deed, we can continually link what happens in the classroom to student learning.

Revising key indicators of the standards that guide our programs, clarifying goals and objectives for our classes, embracing best practices for instruction, and implementing multiple methods of assessment that reveal student growth, thus enabling us to use the data to shape our own practices, are steps that increase our effectiveness. We can draw on our own research to collaborate with colleagues and others who are also deeply invested in issues of student learning, and we can situate ourselves in the profession, resourcefully learning and doing as much as we possibly can to be the kinds of teachers who truly make a difference.

The issue is multifaceted and complex, complicated by political rhetoric, finger pointing, and a testing system run amock. As our educational system adjusts to a standards-based model of individualized instruction and increased accountability, and as the standards that guide our efforts continue to evolve, effective teachers continue to focus on what is essential, even as methods for getting there continue to change.

Conclusion

Florida Standards: A Handbook for Teaching in the Sunshine State was designed to serve as an introduction to Florida's standards and how to effectively meet them. Intended to support readers interested in improving curriculum and instruction, the book was written primarily as a supplementary resource for teacher education programs in Florida and for professional development courses designed to help candidates meet requirements for alternative certification.

In light of the increased accountability for student learning, and in the current climate of FCAT, teachers need discussions that include the hard realities, and teacher education programs need references that will support their own efforts to document candidate learning about student learning.

As the movement to connect teaching to learning and the push for increased student competency continue to require teachers to teach at higher levels and with genuine skill, many questions and issues remain. More than ever, teachers face big challenges, frustration, and controversy (Resnick & Zurawsky, 2005), but as the *Sunshine State Standards* and other guidelines continue to be revised, Florida teachers will continue to adjust to meet the latest mandates. Teachers will continue to focus on their students.

Hopefully, as a beginning K–12 teacher, an individual striving to meet the challenge of alternative certification at the district or state level, or an educator grappling with curriculum design and strategies for documenting student learning in the state of Florida, you found value in this volume. May you enjoy a career rich in the knowledge that you are a teacher who truly makes a difference.

Glossary

Key terms presented in this book are defined in this glossary. However, because connotations of words shift according to context and over time, and because some of these concepts represent complex ideas, these definitions should not be considered definitive. The following words are defined only as related to usage in Florida Standards: A Handbook for Teaching in the Sunshine State.

Accountability   Establishing expectations for results of teaching and learning, and then holding teachers and students responsible for the outcome.

Affective Domain   One of three domains of learning, pertaining to dispositions, values, appreciation, and feelings. Difficult to teach and assess, the affective domain is a high-level, lifelong form of learning. Becoming a person who enjoys writing is an example of affective growth.

Alignment   A type of decision making. In order to know if students are learning, teachers must align, or choose, specific assessments matched to the goals and objectives of each lesson. Teachers also match lesson activities to lesson objectives and align any special accommodations to the student's needs.

Assessment   The most important tool used by effective teachers. It is *not* the same as testing or grading. Good assessment is continuous, careful monitoring of student learning and is used to inform every decision a teacher makes.

Benchmarks   Define performance at developmental or grade levels.

Content Standards   Define learning outcomes in academic subjects or disciplines.

Criterion-Referenced Test (CRT)   A CRT, like the FCAT, measures student learning against a set of established traits or criteria. Scores are reported that reference a student's accomplishment compared to the standards.

Declarative Domain   One of three domains of learning, pertaining to facts, knowledge of the subject, identification, and recall. At the lowest level of Bloom's taxonomy, this is the easiest aspect of learning to teach and learn.

Knowing how to define *writing* is an example of this kind of learning.

Delivery Models   Methods of instructional delivery range from transmitting information (lecture) to independent inquiry, role playing, and collaborative problem solving.

Diagnostic Assessment   Diagnostic assessments, such as pretests, surveys, interviews, observation, and any prior examination of student work, can serve to diagnose or determine students' prior knowledge and skills. With such information, teachers can then adjust their plans or make modifications for individual needs.

Florida Comprehensive Assessment Test (FCAT)   This large-scale standardized test, mandated by the state legislature, is designed to assess the academic ability of Florida's students. It is administered annually. The scores are used to assess student achievement of the *Sunshine State Standards*.

Florida Educator Accomplished Practices (*FEAP*)   Subtitled "*Competencies for Teachers of the Twenty-First Century,*" this generic set of 12 teaching proficiencies serves as the standards for teacher professional development in Florida.

Florida Teacher Certification Exam (FTCE)   Passing this licensure test, mandated and administered by the Florida Department of Education, is required of *all* persons seeking teaching certification in the state of Florida.

Formal Assessment   Formal assessment methods, such as rubrics and scoring guides, represent structured evaluation in a uniform manner that links specified outcomes to, say, the completed project. Formal assessment documents student progress in writing and therefore is especially helpful for offering concrete feedback to students.

Formative Assessment Used during the lesson, formative assessments are designed to keep forming or shaping the learning and to monitor the process of student learning.

Goals Educational goals are broadly structured long-term learning outcomes. Large in scope, goals require extended time and repeated teaching to achieve.

Informal Assessment Methods of monitoring the process of student learning that occur continuously, almost naturally, during teaching include asking students questions, probing students' thinking, watching their body language and attitudes, and moving around the room paying close attention to student participation.

Norm-Referenced Test (NRT) An NRT test, like the SAT 10, measures student learning against the scores of other students. Scores are reported that reference a student's accomplishments compared to those of others who have taken the same test.

Objectives Educational objectives focus specifically on learning outcomes, usually taught in a single lesson or series of lessons conducted in a relatively brief period of time.

Procedural Domain One of three domains of learning, pertaining to skills and performances, requiring learners to apply declarative knowledge in order to do something. Knowing how to write is an example of this kind of learning.

Reflection A search for understanding, a process of inquiry that guides teachers to constantly analyze and use information about the teaching and learning experiences. Reflective teachers thoughtfully plan in advance of teaching (reflection-on-action), readily monitor and adjust their plans while teaching (reflection-in-action), and consider the results of their work after teaching (reflection-on-action).

Rubric Another name for a wide range of scoring guides, used for formative response or summative evaluation. Holistic or analytic, a rubric can even be a simple checklist outlining criteria for products or processes.

Standards Generally, statements of learning that detail what students should know or be able to do. Standards may specify certain content or discipline knowledge, specific skill or performance competence, or ideal attitudes and conditions necessary to achieve the desired learning. Standards can be written at the national state, district, or school level.

Standards-based educational system In a standards-based model, the focus of teaching is on student learning. Teaching begins with identifiable objectives or standards that name what students will learn and ends with a form of summative assessment. In between, constant attention is paid to student progress as teachers monitor and adjust the learning process to enable all students to achieve the standards.

Summative Assessment Assessments at the end of the lesson or teaching unit that summarize or evaluate what has been accomplished. Summative assessments are usually created for each objective and thus provide insight into the degree to which the lesson succeeded in helping all students gain the desired knowledge, skill, and belief.

Sunshine State Standards Florida's version of statewide learning standards for students, which are disseminated to all schools to define what Florida students should know and be able to do at certain stages throughout PreK–12 grade levels.

Teacher Work Sample Methodology A process for documenting the teacher's thinking during the learning process. It situates the teaching in a specific context and then utilizes data from prelesson, postlesson, and daily assessments to analyze the impact on learners.

Triangulation The process of collecting reliable data, avoiding the use of just one source of evidence to make student learning visible. Choosing at least three sources of data allows reflective teachers to know better what is happening in the lives of their students. The information gathered is interpreted in order to make formative decisions, supporting the learning process well before it ends.

References

Anderson, L. W. (1991). *Increasing teacher effectiveness.* Paris: UNESCO, International Institute for Educational Planning.

Batten, M., Marland, P., & Khamis, M. (1993). *Knowing how to teach well.* Melbourne, Australia: ACER.

Beerens, D. R. (2000). *Evaluating teachers for professional growth: Creating a culture of motivation and learning.* Thousand Oaks, CA: Corwin Press.

Beers, K. (2004). From many to one. *Voices from the Middle, 11*(4), 4–5.

Bickmore, S. T., Smagorinsky, P., & O'Donnell-Allen, C. (2005). Tensions between traditions: The role of contexts in learning to teach. *English Education, 38*(1), 23–52.

Bissex, G. L. (1980). *Gyns at work: A child learns to write and read.* Cambridge, MA: Harvard University Press.

Blackwell, S. (1997, March). *The dilemma of standards-driven reform.* Paper presented at the annual meeting of the Conference on College Composition and Communication, Phoenix, AZ.

Brancarosa, G., & Snow, C. E. (2004). *Reading next: A vision for action and research in middle and high school literacy.* A report from the Carnegie Corporation of New York. Washington, DC: Alliance for Excellent Education.

Britton, J. (1982). The speaker. In G. M. Pradl (Ed.), *Prospect and retrospect* (pp. 71–79). Montclair, NJ: Boynton/Cook.

Bullard, B. (1998, November). *Teacher self-evaluation.* Paper presented at the annual meeting of the Mid-South Educational Research Association, New Orleans.

Cavanaugh, T. (2002). Assistive technology: Tools to improve instruction. *Florida Educational Leadership, 3*(1), 12–16.

Cawelti, G. (Ed.). (1995). *Handbook of research on improving student achievement.* Arlington, VA: Educational Research Service.

Cochran-Smith, M. (2003). Learning and unlearning: The education of teacher educators. *Teaching and Teacher Education, 19*(1), 5–28.

Cochran-Smith, M. (2005). The new teacher education: For better or for worse? *Educational Researcher, 34*(7), 3–17.

Cohen, D. K. (1995). What is the system in systemic reform? *Educational Researcher, 24*(9), 11–17.

Copeland, M. (2005). *Socratic circles: Fostering critical and creative thinking in middle and high school.* Portland, ME: Stenhouse.

Corio, J. (2003). Exploring literacy on the Internet. *The Reading Teacher, 56*(5), 458–464.

Creemers, B. (1994). *The effective classroom.* London: Cassell.

Dangel, J. R., & Guyton, E. M. (2005). *Research on alternative and non-traditional education: Teacher education handbook XIII.* Lanham, MD: Association of Teacher Educators.

Daniels, H., & Bizar, M. (1998). *Methods that matter: Six structures for best practice classrooms.* York, ME: Stenhouse.

Danielson, C. (1996). *Enhancing professional practice: A framework for teaching.* Alexandria, VA: Association for Supervision and Curriculum Development.

Darling-Hammond, L. (1996). Restructuring schools for high performance. In S. H. Fuhrinan & J. A. O'Day (Eds.), *Rewards and reform: Creating educational incentives that work* (pp. 144–194). San Francisco: Jossey-Bass.

Darling-Hammond, L. (1998). Standards for assessing teaching effectiveness are key: A response to Schalock, Schalock, and Myton. *Phi Delta Kappan, 79*(6), 471–472.

Darling-Hammond, L. (1999). *Reshaping teaching policy, preparation, and practice: Influences of the National Board for Professional Teaching Standards.* Washington, DC: Office of Educational Research and Improvement.

Darling-Hammond, L., & Youngs, P. (2002). Defining "highly qualified teachers": What does "scientifically-based research" actually tell us? *Educational Researcher, 31*(9), 13–25.

De Kock, A., Sleegers, P., & Voeten, M. J. M. (2004). New learning and the classification of learning environments in secondary education. *Review of Educational Research, 74*(2), 141–170.

Delbridge, K. M. (2002). Standards room only! Taking literacy beyond the classroom. *Voices from the Middle, 10*(1), 41–46.

DelMonte, K. (2002). School advisory councils ten years on: Involving stakeholders in school improvement decisions. *Florida Educational Leadership, 3*(1), 46–52.

Dewey, J. (1963). *Experience and education.* New York: Scribner.

Dykema, K. (May/June 2002). How schools fail kids and how they could be better: An interview with Ted Sizer. *Nexxus Journal.* Retrieved March 2004 from *http://www.nexuspub.com/articles/2002/May2002/interview1.htm.*

Eggen, P. D., & Kauchak, D. P. (2006). *Strategies and models for teachers: Teaching content and thinking skills.* Boston: Pearson.

Eisner, E. (1998). *The kind of schools we need.* Portsmouth, NH: Heinemann.

Erb, T. (2002). Achievement: What tests test or something grander? *Voices from the Middle, 10*(1), 4.

Ericsson, P. F. (2005). Raising the standards for standards: A call for definitions. *English Education, 37*(3), 223–243.

Falk, B., & Ort, S. (1998). Sitting down to score: Teacher learning through assessment. *Phi Delta Kappan, 80*(1), 59–64.

Ferdig, R. E., & Trammell, K. D. (2004). Content delivery in the "Blogoshere." *T.H.E. Journal, 31*(7), 12–20.

Fisher, T. E. (1986). Achievement testing in Florida. Document prepared for the Office of Technology Assessment, Tallahassee, FL.

Florida Department of Education. (2005). *Revising the Sunshine State Standards.* A PowerPoint presentation given at a meeting to revise the standards in Tallahassee FL, July 28.

Florida Education Standards Commission. (1996). Florida educator accomplished practices: *Preprofessional competencies for teachers of the 21st century.* Retrieved April 2004 from *http://www.myfloridaeducation.com/dpe/publications/preprofessional4-99.pdf.*

Freiberg, H. J., & Driscoll, A. (2005). *Universal teaching strategies.* Boston: Pearson.

French, D. (2003). A new vision of authentic assessment to overcome the flaws in high stakes testing. *Middle School Journal, 35*(1), 14–23.

Fu, D. (2004). Teaching ELL students in regular classrooms at the secondary level. *Voices from the Middle, 11*(4), 8–15.

Fuhrman, S. H. (1999). *The new accountability* (CPRE Research Report RB-27). Philadelphia: University of Pennsylvania, Consortium for Policy Research in Education.

Gardner, H. (1999). *Intelligence reframed: Multiple intelligences for the twenty-first century.* New York: Basic Books.

Goddard, R. D., Hoy, W. K., & Hoy, A. W. (2004). Collective efficacy beliefs: Theoretical developments, empirical evidence, and future directions. *Educational Researcher, 33*(3), 1–13.

Goodlad, J. (1984). *A place called school.* New York: McGraw-Hill.

Goswami, D., & Stillman, P. R. (1987). *Reclaiming the classroom: Teacher research as an agency for change.* Upper Montclair, NJ: Boynton/Cook.

Gunter, M. A., Estes, T. H., & Schwab, J. (1999). *Instruction: A models approach.* Boston: Allyn & Bacon.

Herrell, A. L. (2000). *Fifty strategies for teaching English language learners.* Upper Saddle River, NJ: Merrill/Prentice Hall.

Heywood, J. (2000). *Assessment in higher education: Student learning, teaching, programmes and institutions.* London: Jessica Kingsley.

Hilliard, A. (2000). Standards: Decoy or quality control? In K. Swope & B. Milner (Eds.), *Failing our kids: Why the testing craze won't fix our schools* (pp. 64–69). Milwaukee: Rethinking Schools Publication.

Holdzkom, D. (1999, April). *Be careful what you ask for: The impact of an accountability system on student achievement, school achievement and teachers.* Paper presented at the annual meeting of the American Educational Research Association, Montreal.

Hunter Quartz, K., & the TEP Research Group (2003). "Too angry to leave": Supporting new teachers' commitment to transform urban schools. *Journal of Teacher Education, 54*(2), 99–111.

Hurt, J. (2003). *Taming the standards: A commonsense approach to higher student achievement, K–12.* Portsmouth, NH: Heinemann.

Ingersoll, R. M. (2001). *Teacher turnover, teacher shortages, and the organization of schools* (CTP Research Report). Seattle: University of Washington, Center for the Study of Teaching and Policy.

Jago, C. (2002). Standards in California: A magical realist view. *Voices from the Middle, 10*(1), 27–30.

Kanstoroom, M., & Finn, C. E. (Eds.). (1999). *Better teachers, better schools.* Washington, DC: The Thomas B. Fordham Foundation.

Kottler, E., Kottler, J. A., & Kottler, C. J. (1998*). Secrets for secondary school teachers: How to succeed in your first year.* Thousand Oaks, CA: Corwin Press.

Kysilka, M. (2005). So what about the FCAT? *Florida Educational Leadership, 5*(2), 28–29.

Landgraf, K. M. (2005). *It's time to act on high school reform.* Retrieved October 22, 2005, from the Educational Testing Service Web site on the issues of teacher quality: *http://www.ets.org*

Lashway, L. (1999). *Holding schools accountable for achievement.* Washington, DC: Office of Educational Research and Improvement.

Linn, R. L. (2000). Assessments and accountability. *Educational Researcher, 29*(2), 4–16.

Lionni, L. (1968). *Swimmy.* New York: Pantheon.

Locke, E. A., & Latham, G. P. (1990). *A theory of goal setting and task performance.* Upper Saddle River, NJ: Prentice Hall.

Lunenberg, M., & Korthagen, F. A. J. (2003). Teacher educators and student-directed learning. *Teaching and Teacher Education, 19*(1), 29–44.

Lyon, G. E. (1989). *Together.* New York: Orchard Books.

Marzano, R. J. (2003). *What works in schools: Translating research into action.* Alexandria, VA: Association for Supervision and Curriculum Development.

McElroy, E. (2005). NCLB's unintended consequences. *On Campus, 24*(8), 2.

McMillan, J. H. (2001). *Classroom assessment: Principles and practice for effective teaching.* Boston: Allyn & Bacon.

Mentkowski, M. (2000). *Learning that lasts: Integrating learning, development, and performance in college and beyond.* San Francisco: Jossey-Bass.

Miller, R. I. (1999). *Major American higher education issues and challenges in the 21st century.* London: Jessica Kingley.

Moulthrop, D., Calegari, N. C., & Eggers, D. (2005). *Teachers have it easy: The big sacrifices and small salaries of America's teachers.* New York: New Press.

Myers, M. (1996). *Changing our minds: Negotiating English and literacy.* Urbana, IL: National Council of Teachers of English.

National Council for Accreditation of Teacher Education. (1999, December 16). *Proposed NCATE 2000 unit standards.* Washington, DC: Author.

No Child Left Behind Act of 2001, Pub. L. No. 107-110, 115 Stat. 1425 (2002).

Olson, S., & Loucks-Horsley, S. (2000). *Inquiry and the National Science Education Standards: A guide for teaching and learning.* Committee on the Development of an Addendum to the National Science Education Standards on Scientific Inquiry, Washington, DC: National Research Council.

Papademetrious, L. (2005). *Sixth-grade glommers, norks, and me.* New York: Hyperion.

Peterson, B., & Salas, K. D. (2004). Working effectively with English language learners. In *The new teacher book* (pp. 220–224). Milwaukee: Rethinking Schools Ltd.

Popham, W. J. (1999). *Classroom assessment: What teachers need to know.* Boston: Allyn & Bacon.

Popham, W. J. (2005). Is The FCAT instructionally supportive? *Florida Educational Leadership, 5*(2), 24–27.

Postal, L. (2004, January 12). Testing of disabled stirs debate. *Sentinel* (Orlando), p. A1.

Rankin, J. A. (Ed.). (1999). *Handbook on problem-based learning.* New York: Forbes Custom Publishers.

Reeves, D. B. (2004). *Accountability for learning: How teachers and school leaders can take charge.* Alexandria, VA: Association for Supervision and Curriculum Development.

Reinke, R. A. (1998). *Challenging the mind, touching the heart: Best assessment practices.* Thousand Oaks, CA: Corwin Press.

Resnick, L. B., & Klopfer, L. E. (Eds.). (1996). *Toward the thinking curriculum: Current cognitive research.* Alexandria, VA: American Association for Supervision and Curriculum Development.

Resnick, L. B., & Zurawsky, C. (2005). Standards-based reform and accountability: Getting back on course. *American Educator, 29*(1), 8–19.

Sagor, R. (1992). *How to conduct collaborative action research.* Alexandria, VA: American Association for Supervision and Curriculum Development.

Sarason, S. B. (2004). *And what do YOU mean by learning?* Portsmouth, NH: Heinemann.

Schön, D. A. (1984). *The reflective practitioner.* New York: Basic Books.

Selber, S. A. (2004). *Multiliteracies for a digital age.* Carbondale: Southern Illinois University Press.

Sewell, A. M. (1997). Accountability and teacher education. *National Forum, 77*(1).

Shepard, L. A. (2000). The role of assessment in a learning culture. *Educational Researcher, 29*(7), 4–14.

Simmons, S. A. (2005). Shortcuts to a meaningful career. *Action in Teacher Education, 27*(1), 36–44.

Sizer, T. (1996). *Horace's hope.* New York: Houghton Mifflin.

Smith, F. (1998). *The book of learning and forgetting.* New York: Teachers College Press.

Spandel, V., & Stiggins, R. J. (1990). *Creating writers: Linking assessment and writing instruction.* New York: Longman.

Stiggins, R. J. (1997). *Student-centered classroom assessment* (2nd ed.). Columbus, OH: Merrill/Prentice Hall.

Stiggins, R. J. (1999). Assessment, student confidence, and school success. *Phi Delta Kappan, 81*(3), 191–198.

Stiggins, R. J. (2001). *Student-involved classroom assessment* (3rd ed.). Columbus, OH: Merrill/Prentice Hall.

Strasser, T. (2000). *Give a boy a gun.* New York: Simon & Schuster Books for Young Readers.

Stronge, J. H. (1997). *Evaluating teaching: A guide to current thinking and best practice.* Thousand Oaks, CA: Corwin Press.

Stronge, J. H. (2002). *Qualities of effective teachers.* Alexandria, VA: Association for Supervision and Curriculum Development.

Stronge, J. H., & Ostrander, L. (1997). Client surveys in teacher evaluation. In J. Stronge (Ed.), *Evaluating teaching* (pp. 129–161). Thousand Oaks, CA: Corwin Press, Inc.

Stronge, J. H., Tucker, P. D., & Hindman, J. L. (2004). *Handbook for qualities of effective teaching.* Alexandria, VA: Association for Supervision and Curriculum Development.

Sturtevant, E. G., & Linek, W. M. (2004). *Content literacy: An inquiry-based case approach.* Upper Saddle River, NJ: Pearson.

Suárez-Orozco, C., & Suárez-Orozco, M. M. (2001). *Children of immigration.* Cambridge, MA: Harvard University Press.

Swaim, S. (2005). Time for serious problem solving. *Middle Ground, 8*(4). Retrieved June 2005 from *http://www.nmsa.org/Publications/MiddleGround/ April2005/tabid/112Default.aspx.*

Swope, K., & Miner, B. (2000). *Failing our kids: Why the testing craze won't fix our schools.* Milwaukee: Rethinking Schools Ltd.

Thoreau, H. D. (1995). *Walden.* New York: Dover.

Vygotsky, L. (1978). *Mind in society: The development of higher psychological processes.* Cambridge, MA: Harvard University Press.

Walberg, H. (2003). Real accountability. In Paul Peterson (Ed.), *Our schools and our future: Are we still at risk?* (pp. 305–328). Stanford, CA: Hoover Institution Press.

Wallace, R. M. (2004). A framework for understanding teaching with the Internet. *American Educational Research Journal, 41*(2), 447–488.

Walters, S. (2004). So what is a teacher union anyway? In K. Salas, S. Walters, & D. Weiss (Eds.), *The new teacher book* (pp. 220–224). Milwaukee: Rethinking Schools Publication.

Wayne, A. J., & Youngs, P. (2003). Teacher characteristics and student achievement: A review. *Review of Educational Research, 73*(1), 89–122.

Wiggins, G. (1996). Embracing accountability. *New Schools, New communities, 12*(2), 4–10.

Wiggins, G., & McTighe, J. (1998). *Understanding by design.* Alexandria, VA: Association for Supervision and Curriculum Development.

Wong, H. K., & Wong, R. (2004). *The first days of school: How to be an effective teacher.* Mountain View, CA: Harry K. Wong.

Wood, S. N. (2002). Preamble to continued thinking, interpretation, and reflection within a teacher work sample. In G. Girod (Ed.), *Connecting teaching and learning: A handbook for teacher educators on teacher work sample methodology* (pp. 263–286). Washington, DC: American Association of the Colleges of Teacher Education.

Wood, S. N. (2005). Mapping school geographies: Teaching and learning in unsafe spaces. *Journal of School Violence, 4*(1), 71–89.

Wright, V., Barron, A. E., & Kromrey, J. D. (1999). Preparing students for high-stakes testing in Florida. *Florida Journal of Educational Research, 39*(1), 79–94.

Yinger, R. J. (2005). A public politics for a public profession. *Journal of Teacher Education, 56*(3), 285–290.

Young, E. (2002). *Seven blind mice.* New York: Penguin Putnam Books.

Zemelman, S., Daniels, H., & Hyde, A. (1998). *Best practice: New standards for teaching and learning in America's schools.* Portsmouth, NH: Heinemann.

Name Index

Subject Index